Voices of Beginning Teachers

Visions and Realities

Voices of Beginning Teachers

Visions and Realities

RICHARD H. DOLLASE

Teachers College, Columbia University
New York and London

Published by Teachers College Press, 1234 Amsterdam Avenue
New York, NY 10027

Library of Congress Cataloging-in-Publication Data

Dollase, Richard H.
    Voices of beginning teachers : visions and realities / Richard H.
    Dollase.
        p.   cm.
    Includes bibliographical references and index.
    ISBN 0-8077-3192-7
    1. First year teachers — United States — Case studies.   2. Teaching —
Social aspects — Case studies.   3. Teachers — Training of — United
States.   I. Title.
    LB2844.1.N4D65   1992
    3371.1′02 — dc20   92-13409

    ISBN 0-8077-3192-7 (pbk.)

Printed on acid-free paper
Manufactured in the United States of America
99 98 97 96 95 94 93 92   8 7 6 5 4 3 2 1

To Bobbie

Contents

Foreword

One cannot help but wonder, amidst the clamor and commotion of educational reform, if we are anywhere near being able to grasp what is perhaps most essential for the continuous renewal of schooling. Can this nation attract the well-educated, the resourceful, the vigorous young to the profession of teaching? Can it hold them there by actively nourishing their own growth, which is essential to that of their students, and by supporting more experienced teachers in their efforts to provide encouragement and guidance to novices joining their ranks? If the answer to these questions remains predominantly negative, no reform is likely to correct the predicament of stagnant schools and lackluster student performance.

Let us pursue the matter a step further by asking how the predicament looks from the perspective of a potentially great teacher who might or might not elect to teach as a career. Can the transition into the classroom be fashioned so that it connects vitally with the dreams of those who choose to teach, not only respecting their needs but truly building upon the lifelong education to which they have committed themselves? If not, the reforms of our time are destined for swift passage to oblivion.

Richard Dollase gives cause for hope that these questions can be answered in the affirmative. His book, *Voices of Beginning Teachers: Visions and Realities*, brings the beginning teacher's rite of passage into extraordinarily clear focus. This study also brings an unusual perspective to the problem. Dollase usefully compares his findings with those of other works in the literature on teaching, but he shifts the perspective by focusing on beginning teachers with strong liberal arts backgrounds from select colleges and universities. He asks, in effect, what happens when the most highly educated young people in the nation make their transition to classroom teaching. The book interprets what can be learned from their experience so that it might be possible in the future to draw more liberally educated teachers into the profession.

This is a challenging, strategic perspective. It does more than tinker with professional requirements and procedures in the name of reform. Dollase asks for a great deal more, no less than that we rethink the nature of the problem itself, aiming not just for higher standards and a restructured workplace, but for a whole way of life in which beginning teachers can activate their vision of education in the settings where they choose to teach.

The strength of the book is that it offers such a perspective, unabashedly idealistic, with a keen practical eye toward the conditions of teaching. Based on careful analysis and using examples scrupulously grounded in empirical observation, the study gives voice to the aspirations of some of the nation's most distinguished beginning teachers and their mentors. Anyone wishing to improve schooling in this country can profit from listening to what they have to say as recorded and interpreted in Dollase's timely research.

Thomas James
Brown University

Acknowledgments

I should like to thank a number of individuals who have contributed to the writing of this work on beginning teachers. First, I wish to thank the first-year and veteran teachers who participated in the study. All of these educators whose individual and collective voices are at the heart of this book were open, warm, and gracious to me. From Middlebury College, I should like to express my appreciation to Betty Thurber, my colleague in the Teacher Education Program, who read and reread each draft for stylistic consistency; to Rudi Haerle, professor of sociology, who provided expert advice on interpreting the statistical evidence; and to Carol Sampson, my department's secretary, who helped type and photocopy the many drafts of the work. I should also like to thank my Brown University colleague, Thomas James, associate professor of education. He both critiqued the manuscript and graciously provided a foreword to the book. Many editors at Teachers College Press provided skilled editorial assistance. Ron Galbraith, an acquisitions editor who died at a young age before the book was published, provided encouragement and concrete suggestions for improving the manuscript at its earliest stage. Sarah Biondello, executive acquisitions editor, helped me in "learning the ropes" of Teachers College Press editorial procedures and policies and in speeding along the publication of the manuscript. Susan Liddicoat, developmental editor, provided careful reading and superb editorial comment and advice. And finally, my deepest appreciation to my wife, Roberta Dollase. She critiqued each version of the book and put up with it all.

Voices of Beginning Teachers

Visions and Realities

CHAPTER 1

Introduction

In Robert Bolt's *A Man for All Seasons* (1962), this conversation takes place between Sir Thomas More and Richard Rich, a younger associate still searching for his professional identity.

> More: Why not be a teacher? You'd be a fine teacher. Perhaps even a great one.
> Rich: And if I was, who would know it?
> More: You, your pupils, your friends, God. Not a bad public, that. . . . Oh, and a quiet life. (p. 6)

Clearly, the need to attract able individuals into teaching is an age-old problem. As More points out, the calling certainly has its benefits, yet many people of talent remain skeptical. Today, as in the past, the teacher's role is critical to the future prosperity and well-being of our society. However, even with the recent upturn in the number of young and older adults training for a career in education, there are still not enough well-qualified teachers in the pipeline. Many of our finest students who are contemplating teaching in elementary and secondary schools are ambivalent if not conflicted. While altruistic and eager to make a difference, these individuals are also troubled about the sacrifices they must make to devote their lives to helping educate and nurture the next generation of Americans. With the anticipated shortage of teachers now on the near horizon, the entry into the profession of many of these well-prepared and idealistic individuals is needed to replenish the ranks of an aging teaching corps and to help rejuvenate and reform the profession. Is teaching a rewarding vocation? Are the sacrifices worth the effort? One way to answer that set of substantive questions is to focus on those highly qualified, liberally educated individuals who are beginning their careers as teachers.[1] As they might put it, what is the "stuff" of teaching in the real world of the schools?

---

1. In a recent report of the Association of American Colleges (Johnson & Associates, 1989), the definition of a highly qualified teacher is "a broadly educated individual who has command of both the subjects to be taught and of the ways which they can be taught effectively to the range of students he or she will be teaching" (p. 10).

While there have been many studies of beginning teachers, few, if any, have focused in depth on the liberal arts graduates from select colleges and universities who pursue careers in secondary school teaching. How do these novices—some of the very best and brightest young Americans—perceive, adapt to, and manage their new role as classroom teachers? What is life like for them in schools? What problems, dilemmas, triumphs, and opportunities do they confront as they learn to teach and as they forge their professional identities as classroom instructors? Moreover, given that most of these liberally educated teachers have a minimum of coursework in the field of education, how do they perceive their initial full-time teaching experience? In what ways are they prepared for the rigor and challenge of classroom teaching? What do they think is good teaching and what specifically are their criteria of good practice? How do other professionals in their schools view their effectiveness? Finally, what new or more formal collegial relationships need to be established to promote the adult development and the professional growth of these beginners? Can such innovative programs as reflective mentoring of beginning teachers by experienced colleagues help retain in teaching more well-qualified, liberally educated teachers and, in the process, also help lead to the greater professionalization of teaching itself?

The remainder of this introduction is divided into two principal sections. In the first the liberal preparation of beginning teachers is discussed. In the second section the research protocol of the beginning teacher study is described.

THE LIBERAL PREPARATION OF TEACHERS

Above all see to it that he is a seeker and a student of that study by which he might be able to learn and find out who will give him the capacity and the knowledge to distinguish the good and the bad life, and so everywhere and always choose the better from among those that are possible. (Plato/ Socrates, *The Republic*, 628c; Bloom, 1968, p. 301)

At liberal arts institutions such as Brown University and Middlebury College, teacher preparation is founded on and grows out of the study of the liberal arts. In 1983 Barnard College, Brandeis University, Brown University, Connecticut College, Dartmouth College, Middlebury College, Mount Holyoke College, Princeton University, Smith College, Swarthmore College, the University of Pennsylvania, Vassar College, Wellesley College, Wesleyan University, and Yale University formed the Consortium for Excellence in Teacher Education (CETE). Harvard University joined the Consortium in 1985. The 16 CETE institutions share common concerns and a general philosophical perspective toward the liberal preparation of prospective teachers.

As the quotation above suggests, the Consortium members view teaching as a moral craft, and our role as one of helping to "integrate theory and practice and to cultivate thoughtful, analytic practitioners" (Travers & Sacks, 1987, p. 9). It is a humanistic, inquiry-oriented approach to teacher education that is informed by two principles: development and integration. A third tenet of many CETE institutions is the working assumption that "small is beautiful," especially in terms of the development and nurturance of a community of reflective practitioners. Because CETE members advocate high "standards without standardization," we also endorse multiple pathways to teacher preparation, and each of our programs has a distinctive thematic emphasis. To paraphrase *Voltaire's Candide* (Gay, 1963): Each of us cultivates our own small garden (p. 299).

Furthermore, like all good preparation programs, CETE programs are informed by "best practice" as articulated by the education research community and carried out by effective teachers in the schools. Finally, the various Consortium member institutions are influenced by and must be responsive to the regulation and mandates of their particular state department of education or state legislature.

Development

The Consortium programs are designed to promote continuity and reflection about the profession of teaching. Through a gradual, sequential process, prospective teachers gain increasing understanding of the teaching and learning processes. School-based practica, including classroom observations, tutoring, internships, field research, and student teaching, promote a "structured role transition—from being a student to becoming a teacher" (Travers & Sacks, 1987, p. 9). The central importance of such an experiential, "hands-on, minds-on," school-based process is articulated in *Teacher Education and the Liberal Arts*, the CETE position paper.

> During the process students have numerous opportunities for serious reflection about both the ideals and realities of the teaching profession. They take on responsibility for increasingly open-ended and complex teaching tasks, and they systematically analyze the interactions between their teaching methods and the learning style of their pupils. The placement of practice teachers is individualized to ensure, as far as possible, that the students' experiences are empowering rather than either overwhelming or insufficiently challenging. (Travers & Sacks, 1987, pp. 8–9)

In practice, prospective teachers at CETE institutions take between six and nine education courses: one or two foundations of education courses, two or more methods courses, and student teaching that is the equivalent of three or four course credits. Because of the multifaceted nature of the elementary school curriculum, students in an elementary school preparation program generally take one or two more methods courses than students pursuing secondary school teacher licensure. Normally, the prepracticum courses have a field-based component involving classroom observation, or tutoring and assisting a teacher in the classroom.

The Middlebury College undergraduate teacher education program and the Brown University Master of Arts in Teaching (MAT) Program curricula typify the programmatic course requirements for prospective teachers at CETE institutions and many other liberal arts colleges and universities. At Middlebury College, a prospective elementary school teacher takes eight related courses, including child psychology, language arts methods, science and mathematics methods, arts methods, and a curriculum development seminar taught concurrently with a full-time, 13-week student teaching practicum (three course credits). A prospective secondary school teacher's curriculum consists of seven courses: a critical issues of education or adolescent development elective; a reading and study skills methods course; a full-time, month-long winter term field experience internship; and a special methods seminar in the subject area, offered concurrently with a full-time, 13-week student teaching practicum (three course credits).

At Brown University, graduate students complete a minimum of four education offerings: a foundation of education elective in philosophy, history, or sociology; a psychology of teaching offering; a methods course in teaching the subject matter; and an analysis-of-teaching seminar taught concurrently with student teaching (both for one credit). In addition, MAT students teach in a six-week intensive summer school program that emphasizes Theodore Sizer's (1984) "student-as-worker" principle and is guided by master teachers, some of whom are Coalition of Essential School instructors.

In each case, whether at the undergraduate or graduate level, the teacher education curriculum at these two institutions and a majority of other CETE colleges and universities is based on a "minimalist" design. In learning to teach, prospective teachers need take only those education courses that satisfy state licensure requirements and that provide broad exposure to the field and a deepening working understanding of the principles and procedures of best practice in the classroom. To maximize the number of liberal arts courses in a prospective teacher's undergraduate education, seven of the Consortium institutions, including Brandeis, Harvard, Vassar, and Wellesley, offer tuition-free or low-cost, ninth-semester student teaching programs. Recent graduates are able to return to the campus to undertake student teaching. These programs have grown in popularity and interest since their inception in the mid-1980s. Establishment of such "postgraduate" or four-and-a-half-year programs have attracted more science and foreign language majors who find it difficult to fit in all teaching licensure requirements in the normal four-year undergraduate program.

Integration

At CETE institutions, teacher education faculty strive to integrate the liberal arts perspective in the preparation of their prospective teachers. Employing the concepts, analytical frameworks, and research methodologies of the various liberal arts disciplines, education courses are often interdisciplinary or cross-disciplinary in nature and deal with fundamental questions of educational purpose and practice. As spelled out in the CETE position paper (Travers & Sacks, 1987), the study of education achieves integration between professional and liberal study in two ways.

> First, the study of educational theory, policy and practice is closely linked to investigation of theory, policy and practice in other areas of the liberal arts curriculum; and second, educational theory and practice are investigated together, enabling our students to become theoretically informed and critically aware practitioners. (p. 10)

Liberal arts faculty at many of the CETE institutions also collaborate with the teacher education staff in developing or teaching the program's curriculum. Such cooperation and working partnerships help break down the isolation of the teacher education program from the other departments, and in many students' eyes help raise the perception of teaching as an important public service career. For instance, liberal arts faculty teach foundations of education courses, guest-lecture in education courses, serve on teacher education program steering committees, or, in the case of Wesleyan University, jointly conduct methods seminars in the subject areas with school practitioners. In school–college partnerships such as Middlebury College has established with its local schools and with DeWitt Clinton High School in the Bronx, liberal arts professors also directly work in public schools, guest-lecturing in classes, consulting with teachers, and participating in joint workshops such as one on "Writing Across the Curriculum."

Finally, teacher preparation program staff work hard to integrate theory and practice, particularly during the student teaching practicum. In the concurrent seminar and during the college supervisor–student teacher conferences, the principal focus of conversation is on reflective problem solving. Specifically, through the analysis of cases and critical incidents that grow out of daily teaching experiences, the supervisor and the practice teacher are able to consider alternative pedagogies and to integrate theory and practice by sustained reflection on teaching and learning in the specific context of the student teacher's classroom.

Small Is Beautiful

A characteristic that is true of the undergraduate programs and most of the CETE graduate programs is their small size and close personal contact between faculty and prospective teachers. To paraphrase the subtitle of E.F. Schumacher's (1973) influential economic work, *Small Is Beautiful: Economics as If People Mattered*, CETE programs' motto might well be "Teacher preparation as if teachers mattered." In his chapter on the "Question of Size," Schumacher states:

> For every activity there is a certain appropriate scale, and the more active and intimate the activity, the smaller the number of people that can take part. . . . Take teaching: . . . what are we trying to teach? . . . It then becomes immediately apparent that certain things can only be taught in a very intimate circle. What scale is appropriate? It depends on what we are trying to do. (p. 62)

Clearly, teacher education programs at CETE institutions require a circle of intimacy appropriate to fostering reflective practice in a supportive liberal arts context. Historically, the teacher education programs at most CETE institutions have been relatively small in number of both faculty and student concentrators. For example, staff size ranges from two full-time faculty members at Yale, Swarthmore, and Wellesley and three full-time faculty at Middlebury and Connecticut College to six or seven full-time faculty at Brown and Smith and five full-time faculty and eight part-time staff at the University of Pennsylvania. These staffing numbers are in line with the three-to-five member faculty range that Goodlad (1990, p. 82) found at most liberal arts institutions in his recent national study of teacher education programs.

Annual student teaching enrollments range from about 100 at Harvard to 50 or so at Brown, slightly over 20 at Middlebury and Swarthmore, and 10 to 15 at Princeton and Wellesley. Overall enrollments in the programs vary from over 650 students at the University of Pennsylvania and Smith, 200 to 300 students at Brown, Middlebury, Vassar, and Connecticut College, to a low of 40 to 75 undergraduates at Princeton and Wesleyan. While the faculty to student ratio at these colleges and universities varies yearly, class size is normally 15 to 20, particularly in advanced seminars and the methods and field experiences courses. More important, the college supervision load is usually no more than four to six student teachers each academic semester.

Such small programs with favorable faculty to student ratios allow for the kind of "purpose, push and personalization" that Powell, Farrar, and Cohen (1985, p. 316) state in the *Shopping Mall High School* are crucial ingredients of successful secondary schools and "more committed learning communities" on any level of the American educational system. John Goodlad (1990), too, in his recent work, *Teachers for Our Nation's Schools*, cites a number of factors that are favorable to the education of teachers at liberal arts colleges, including a "strong, shared ethos regarding the priority of general education and the liberal arts" and the "centrality of teaching" (pp. 80–81). As he points out, "In these environments, consistent neglect of teaching is quickly known. There is a considerable degree of student and peer pressure to teach well" (p. 81).

As important, the smallness of the typical CETE program allows for the development and implementation of a well-structured and well-supported student teaching practicum in the schools. Given the limited number of field placements required in the local schools, the practicum experience of student teachers can be well-supervised by the college faculty. For example, at Middlebury and Swarthmore, student teachers are observed weekly in their classrooms. There is also close collaboration between the college supervisor and the cooperating teacher, usually an experienced professional who has worked with student teachers for many years. At Middlebury College the arrangement with school administrators and teachers has been informally structured and has evolved over time in response to changing needs on the part of both the schools and the College. Each semester, cooperating teachers meet with the Teacher Education Program staff to discuss their respective roles and to consider ways to improve the practicum experience. Recently, the public school teachers and teacher educators discussed how to design and implement a new system of evaluation by portfolio of student teachers' performance and teaching competence.

At Brown University, teacher centers have been established in the Providence public schools and one suburban Rhode Island secondary school. The purposes of the centers are to develop a sense of community and shared perspectives among student teachers and their mentors; to promote substantive and sustained collaboration between teacher educators and school practitioners; and to encourage innovative teaching and supervision of student teachers. Brown student teachers are clustered at teaching center schools and are supervised by multiple mentors—the clinical professor, a cooperating teacher, and a coordinating teacher who has served as a cooperating teacher and who is noted for her or his teaching expertise and leadership among the faculty. The teaching centers have their own advisory board, the coordinating secondary school teacher is given one-fifth released time to carry out the duties of the role, and Brown University clinical professors work directly with teachers and secondary students in these schools. Liberal arts professors also teach and consult in the schools. The teaching center sponsors inservice seminars for cooperating teachers based on their perceived needs.

In the Brown and Middlebury programs, experienced teachers receive honoraria ranging from $150 to $500 for their services as cooperating teachers. In addition, these professionals are given library privileges and are able to use such other college facilities as the academic computer center.

New Directions

In recent years, Consortium members have attempted to help first-year teachers by conducting beginning-teacher conferences and establishing beginning teachers' telecommunication networks. Brown University for many years has conducted a beginning-teacher institute that is primarily for independent school teachers but also includes public school teachers. For the past several years, Vassar College has held a one-day, beginning-teacher conference on its campus. Barnard and Swarthmore instituted first-year conferences in 1991. Also in the academic year 1990–91, Middlebury College joined with the other 10 teacher preparation institutions in Vermont to hold a state-wide, beginning-teacher conference on its campus.

In 1986, Harvard University established its Beginning Teachers' Computer Network (or electronic bulletin board and message system), which enables first-year teachers to communicate with the teacher education program staff and with each other at their homes and schools. The network permits graduates from across the country to keep in touch with each other and to provide advice and perspective on the initial year of full-time teaching.

Middlebury College and the other Vermont colleges hope in the near future to establish a beginning teachers' support network that will include both a series of yearly conferences permitting periodic face-to-face contact, and a telecommunications network to provide beginning teachers a daily opportunity to communicate with their teacher education mentors and with each other when they need immediate or short-term help in the classroom.

Finally, like other leading colleges and universities across the country, CETE institutions are establishing (or renewing) school–college/university partnerships, particularly with urban schools. Brown works with the Providence schools, Connecticut College collaborates with the New London schools, Mount Holyoke has entered a partnership with the Northhampton (Massachusetts) schools, Middlebury has a two-year-old partnership with DeWitt Clinton High School in New York City, Wellesley has a long-established working relationship with Boston Latin School, and Yale University has had comprehensive and sustained involvement in the New Haven inner-city schools. All of these initiatives are aimed at helping to improve urban schooling through collaboration based on the principles of equality and respect rather than fiat from above. As they evolve, these urban school partnerships are likely to transform the traditional notion of the teaching task still held in many schools and colleges. From imparting knowledge to students in the standard ways, to practicing innovative problem-based learning, prospective teachers must be involved in "connecting important ideas to diverse learners" (Kennedy, 1991, p. 10). This mission is a complex task that teacher educators at CETE institutions are now wrestling with as they focus their educational mission for the twenty-first century on helping make a difference in our inner-city schools.

THE RESEARCH STUDY

This purposeful study of a small but significant subset of our nation's secondary school teachers examines 28 recent graduates from two teacher education programs, the undergraduate preparation program at Middlebury College and the Master of Arts in Teaching Program at Brown University, over the course of the 1988–89 academic year. In addition, nine other first- or second-year secondary school teachers who received certification at Barnard College, Harvard University, Hunter College, Trinity College, the University of Michigan, and the University of Vermont also participated in the exploratory study. Finally, one first-year teacher, a Yale University graduate, who had not completed a formal certification program but who taught in a public school was included in the study. He is following an alternate route to certification.

Research Protocol

The research study involved the following protocol: Two sets of questionnaires—the first in October/November 1988 and the second in May 1989—were sent to 1987 and 1988 graduates of the various teacher preparation programs. In mid-May, questionnaires were also sent to experienced teachers at the schools of these beginners in order to ascertain how the beginning teachers' workload, schedule, and cycle of teaching compared with those of the veteran teachers and how the novice teachers' problems, challenges, and concerns fit into the larger context of the specific school environment. Cooperating teachers from the Middlebury and Brown teacher education programs were also polled to increase the pool of experienced teachers and to allow for greater insight into how the nature of American schooling and the secondary school classroom shapes and patterns the professional lives of the novice and the veteran teacher alike. In total, questionnaires were received from 25 veteran teachers (14 teachers working in the same schools as the beginning teachers and 11 cooperating teachers).

In reporting, first- and second-year teachers are "lumped" together as beginners, for two reasons. First, an analysis of the data revealed very few significant differences in their respective rankings on the major research questions asked. Second, to gain a broader perspective on the new teachers in the study, it was important to compare them with larger samples of beginners. The major national (Lortie, 1975) and international studies (Veenman, 1984) of beginning teachers that are discussed in this book also combined first- and second-year teachers when reporting their findings on beginning teachers.

Of the 38 beginning teachers (24 first-year teachers and 14 second-year teachers), 20 (13 first-year teachers and seven second-year teachers) were subsequently observed and interviewed in their schools in the New England and New York areas. The teachers' schools were within a 150-mile radius of the Boston area. The classroom observations were not used to assess the teaching effectiveness of the beginning teachers. Rather they served to reveal the beginners' general classroom teaching style and helped give a specific and immediate context to many of the questions asked in the subsequent interview. Observing the beginners before the interview helped make the inexperienced teachers more open and usually elicited from them more detailed responses to the interview questions.

There was an effort to make the sample representative of a variety of school settings and teaching fields. The qualitative data derived from the questionnaires, observations, and interviews made possible the development of four individual case studies of first-year teachers as well as a composite group portrait of the beginning teachers in the context of their school environments.

Case Studies

To illustrate the evolving classroom perspectives of liberally educated beginning teachers, four case studies were created from the observations, interviews, and questionnaire responses of four first-year teachers and their mentors — the experienced teachers, department chairs, and school principals who worked with them during their initial year of teaching. Follow-up interviews were held with the four beginning teachers during spring and summer 1990, their second year of teaching, to obtain additional data for the case studies, particularly in regard to their early teaching experiences.

The case study is useful in helping reveal how individuals feel about their occupations and the institutions in which they work. In anthropologist Bronislaw Malinowski's terms (cited in Hammersley, 1986), "it puts flesh and blood on the skeleton" (p. 190) and helps us get to the realities of human life. These portraits of newcomers constitute Part I of this book.

Demographics

Table 1.1 details the demographics of the sample of beginning teachers. As in other studies of beginning teachers, the vast majority of the 38 novices were in their twenties. However, two teachers were in their late thirties, and one teacher was in her forties. Consistent with the general composition of the middle school and high school teaching staffs, the majority of teachers were women. There were three minority teachers in the sample: a female Hispanic first-year teacher who taught in a large urban school, a male African-American first-year teacher who taught in a suburban school, and a female African-American second-year teacher who taught at an experimental urban school. Almost three-quarters of the beginners taught in public schools, and the others in independent or parochial schools. While the majority of the newcomers worked in suburban school environments, almost a third of the sample found employment in rural schools, particularly in Vermont where Middlebury College is located. Fewer than 20% of the respondents taught in urban schools, most of them in the New York City area. A majority of the new teachers taught in small-school environments. Only four teachers worked in large suburban or urban schools of more than a thousand students.

Most beginners rated their schools as above the national norm, and fewer than 10% of the teachers indicated that their school was below average in the academic achievement of students on standardized tests or percentage of students attending college after graduation. The data suggest that these newcomers managed to find jobs in better than average schools, but the large majority did not teach in the elite suburban schools surrounding Boston or New York City.

Almost two-thirds of the sample of beginning teachers taught the equivalent of five classes daily — the norm in most public schools. Over a quarter of the teachers taught four classes daily but had additional teaching duties most days, such as conducting science labs or tutoring sessions. Of

Table 1.1. Demographics of Study Sample of Beginning Teachers

	Number	Percentage
Personal Characteristics		
Age		
22-25	21	55
26-30	14	36
31-40	2	6
41-50	1	3
Gender		
Male	16	42
Female	22	58
Ethnics/Racial Group		
White	35	92
African-American	2	5
Hispanic	1	3
Schools of Employment		
Type		
Public	28	74
Private	10	26
Environment		
Rural	12	32
Suburban	20	53
Urban	6	16
Level		
Middle school	12	32
High school	26	68
Size		
100-200	1	3
201-500	13	35
501-750	8	21
751-1000	10	26
1001-2000	4	10
2001-3000	2	5
Academic Achievement		
Much above norm	9	24
Slightly above norm	14	37
At national norm	9	24
Slightly below norm	4	10
Much below norm	2	5
Workload		
Students Taught		
32-49	5	13
50-69	8	22
70-89	15	39
90-109	7	18
110-122	3	8

`Table 1.1. *Continued*

	Number	Percentage
Workload (continued)		
Classes Taught		
Five	24	63
Four	10	26
Three or less	4	11
Daily Preparations		
Five	3	8
Four	2	5
Three	14	37
Two	13	34
One	6	16
Teaching Fields		
Humanities		
English	10	26
Social studies	12	32
English & social studies	2	5
Foreign language	2	5
Science & math		
Science	6	16
Math	5	13
Other		
Special education	1	3

the four teachers who taught three or fewer classes, two teachers taught in independent schools, one urban teacher's class load was reduced from five to three classes at midyear, and the other novice taught and counseled at an experimental school. Finally, more than 80% of the teachers had three or fewer preparations daily, close to the norm in most American schools.

The number of students these educators taught daily ranged from a low of 32 students in a New York State boarding school to a high of 122 students in a growing suburban community in Massachusetts. Most teachers in the sample had fewer than 100 students. In fact, only three teachers taught between 110 and 122 students. In general, this low student to teacher ratio in most public as well as private schools is at first somewhat surprising, but it is perhaps reflective of the declining secondary-school-age population in the northeastern suburbs as well as the large number of rural public schools (12) and the small number of large urban or suburban schools (3) in the sample.

Finally, as anticipated, the majority of the beginners in the study were humanities teachers, primarily teaching English or social studies. Traditionally, most of the prospective teachers in liberal arts colleges major in these subject areas. However, there were also six science teachers and five mathematics teachers in the sample, which perhaps reflects the renewed interest of individuals with these majors in undertaking a career in teaching. In fact, all three beginning teachers over the age of 35 were in this group of science and mathematics teachers.

To summarize, while the sample of beginning teachers is atypical in that they graduated from select liberal arts institutions, where they teach is not far different from the majority of American teachers. As is the case at these liberal arts institutions, minority teachers are underrepresented. Likewise, because of the locations where these teachers are employed, such as northern New England, urban schools are also underrepresented but rural and lower middle-class and working-class suburban schools are not. Although most of these teachers feel that their student populations are above average in achievement, their perceptions may have as much to do with the "Lake Wobegon effect" as with actual fact. Except for four or five suburban schools outside the metropolitan areas of Boston and New York City and six urban schools, the majority of the schools in which these beginners teach have a range of students that is reflective of most other schools in predominantly white communities. There is ethnic and social class diversity within almost all of these schools but little racial diversity. For the most part, these newcomers to the profession confront many of the same problems and dilemmas that most other teachers face in public and private secondary schools across the nation.

Throughout this book teaching dilemmas and difficult problems will be used to illustrate what Schön (1983) has termed the "complexity, uncertainty, instability, uniqueness and value conflicts . . . central to the work of professional practice" (p. 14). Beginning teaching in the dynamic world of the secondary school certainly fits this characterization. Each dilemma highlights both the creative tensions and the value conflicts that make classroom teaching challenging, dynamic, and full of personal meaning and significance for the novice as well as the veteran teacher. The voices of these beginning teachers (and some of the experienced teachers) provide eloquent and authentic testimony to the importance and the vital nature of teaching. This testimony also reveals the formative changes occurring in the lives of these newcomers to the profession.

Part I of the book presents four case studies of first-year teachers who describe in their own words their vision—their special sense of mission and their unique and evolving professional identity as classroom teachers. Of the three female teachers portrayed, one teaches English in a rural New England school, the second teaches a foreign language in a suburban high school, and the third teaches science in a large urban secondary school. The science teacher is Hispanic and the other two are white. The male teacher is African-American and teaches in a suburban school setting. Part II focuses on the dynamics and the realities of beginning teaching: its substantive problems, dilemmas, and challenges for all the beginning teachers in the study. It also reveals the beginning teachers' views of teaching, their concerns as professionals, and the mentoring support they receive or need as newcomers to the field of education.

PART I

Portraits of Beginning Teachers: The Vision

On one level, teaching means to impart knowledge and skill. On another level, it is meant "to stimulate, encourage, and support a person's search for meaning" (Westerhoff, 1987, p. 191). In either sense, teaching, in my view, is what "turns on" many of these young professionals whom I interviewed.

The chapters in this part constitute four case studies of first-year teachers. The narratives of these four teachers help illuminate their views of teaching and many of the special qualities that are characteristic of the majority of beginners in this study. The four beginning teachers discuss their first year of teaching and their developing classroom teaching perspective. Perspective is a heuristic concept growing out of the work of George Mead (1938) and other symbolic interactionists. As defined by Becker, Geer, Hughes, and Strauss (1961),

> It is a coordinated set of ideas and actions a person uses in dealing with some problematic situation . . . a person's ordinary way of thinking and acting in such a situation. These thoughts and actions are coordinated in the sense that the actions flow reasonably from the actor's point of view. (p. 34)

Understanding a teacher's perspective helps unlock "the underlying rationale for the person's action"; an individual's personal perspective is "seen by the actor as providing a justification for acting as he does" (p. 34).

Like Lightfoot's (1983) work, *The Good High School*, the underlying goal of the portraits is to "capture the essence: the spirit, tempo and movement" of these beginning teachers' evolving sense of the reality and deeper meaning of their teaching (p. 5). In telling their stories, the focus is on portraying the "insider's view of what is important" and on reporting the beginners' personal mosaics of their teaching mission "from the inside out" (pp. 7, 14). The creation of these portraits is also informed by Kennedy's (1989a) concept of "working knowledge," which "refers to the evolving body of knowledge that practitioners draw on for the varied decisions they make" (p. 2). Such tentative and changing knowledge related to the workplace includes "experiences, research findings, theoretical understandings, myths, folklore, beliefs, and values as well. It is the sum of all ideas that influence practice" (p. 2). Finally, the analysis of these beginning teachers' understanding of their teaching was illuminated by asking them to select a metaphor that best describes their role in the classroom when consciously engaging in the teaching that matters to them (see Tobin, 1990). As Dickmeyer (1989) reminds us, "a metaphor is a characterization of a phenomenon in familiar terms. We use metaphors to grasp intellectually systems that operate in ways quite mysterious to us" (pp. 151–152). For all the research, teaching remains a complex and hard-to-define mode of public and private interaction. Metaphoric analysis helps to unlock in poignant ways how beginners view the role and its existential meaning for them.

To gain further perspective on the beginners and their developing classroom teaching personas, the formal or informal mentor teacher(s), department head, and principal at their respective secondary schools were asked to reflect on the newcomers and to evaluate their strengths and weaknesses as classroom teachers. They were also asked to select the metaphor that best depicted the beginners' teaching style in the classroom.

The four portraits of neophytes are both typical and atypical of the liberally educated graduates who go into teaching. (The names of these first-year teachers have, of course, been changed.) Wendy Light (Chapter 2) is a beginner who teaches English at the middle school level in rural New England. She is also a coach at the secondary school. James Crawford-Williams (Chapter 3), an African-American, is a social studies teacher in a wealthy public high school in Massachusetts. Because he did not complete a teacher education program before entering teaching, he is atypical of the other beginners in the sample but similar to other "Ivy League" teachers in the Teach-for-America Program that was recently established. He is also a lay minister. Elizabeth Alberto (Chapter 4) teaches Spanish at the same Boston-area school as Crawford-Williams. As a *summa cum laude* graduate who studied in Spain for several years, she is the kind of subject-matter specialist that foreign language departments are eager to have as members of their faculty. Finally, Maria Fernandez (Chapter 5) is an Hispanic teacher who taught science her first year in a large urban high school in New York City. She is the single parent of two young adults.

These beginning teachers share in common a desire to make a difference and the will "to give all" in terms of helping their students in and outside of the classroom. They are full of optimism, hope, and creativity. In that sense, while not unique, they are special people who in their role as first-year teachers nurtured and helped enable the next generation of Americans. Of course, like most new teachers, these beginners faced complex and challenging problems in the classroom. During times of such "storm and stress with their adolescent students," they had difficulty coping and they made rookie mistakes. The harsher realities of their (and other beginners') first year of teaching are analyzed in Part II. In these case studies the emphasis is on the neophytes' informing vision and their emerging mission as new professionals. As Joseph Featherstone (1988) states, "Teachers play an important 'liberal' role as the storytellers of the culture" (p. 5). Here are four beginners' stories of what it means to learn to teach and to make a difference in the culture of the classroom itself.

CHAPTER 2

Teacher as Player-Coach: Wendy Light

Wendy Light is a 23-year-old middle school English teacher who was born and raised in Rutland, Vermont. She is tall and athletic in appearance with a winning, outgoing personality. Wendy is the second of four sisters. Her father is a real estate appraiser, and her mother, a kindergarten teacher. They both supported her decision to teach. "Especially my mother, but my father definitely did too," she indicated.

Light depicts herself in high school as a "diligent" student who did not have to work too hard to achieve good grades. "I was," she states, "one of those goody-goody students who always did her homework — maybe the teacher's pet in some instances." As a high school student, Wendy participated in cross-country running, cheerleading, and student council. She graduated from Middlebury College in 1988, where she majored in English and had a minor concentration in teacher education.

Wendy had an early interest in teaching when in grade school. "I used to play teacher at home," she said. Later in high school she gave up her career goal. It was not until her sophomore year in college that she again thought seriously about a career in teaching. Her renewed interest in the profession had a great deal to do with her major, which she found stimulating; with her desire to continue to do something with English after college; and with her wish to work with young people whom she "really enjoys." Her decision was also influenced by an English professor who she says inspired her. She comments, "I saw this teacher teach and I thought, 'Why can't all teaching be like that?'" When asked to describe why the English professor, a poet, was an exemplary role model for her, she said:

> I went in there with the attitude that poetry was just the worst thing that I could ever take. I didn't want to deal with it. But I was actually sad when the course ended. He was just the kind of professor who could get you charged up. The class started at 2:45 in the afternoon, which is probably the worst time for a class to start. Everybody would come in, and by the end of the class all of us were just sitting up on the edge of our seats.

During the class, he was able to point things out and make you look at things in a different way. It was also important to him to hear what you had to say. A lot of teachers just sit up there and spout at you what they know. He would get the class involved, too. Even in a class of 40 or 50, he managed to have a running discussion going as he was lecturing. He was interested, and everything you said counted. He just had such an energy up there, such a presence that he was able to get you right up there with him. He just got everyone involved. If it looked like everyone was falling asleep, he'd make you stand up and jump around for five seconds. He just always had you going.

In her own teaching Wendy attempts to get her students "involved" and to model her method of instruction as much as possible after that of the Middlebury professor. Her teaching style will be discussed more fully in the following sections.

At the beginning of her job search, Wendy was interested in teaching high school English in Montgomery County, Maryland. She had taught tenth graders during her student teaching in the spring semester of her senior year at the local high school in Middlebury.

However, she eventually took a middle school English teaching job at a Grade 7–12 secondary school in northern New England. During her first year of teaching she taught eighth and ninth graders. The public school has about 800 students. Between 35% and 50% of the senior class go on to some form of higher education. In Wendy's view the level of student achievement at the school is at about the national norm. She characterizes the general atmosphere of the school as moderately strict.

During her first year, Wendy taught 87 students in five classes and had between three and four daily preparations. She often put in a 60-hour week or more. In an average week at school, she taught for 20 hours, put 10 hours into lesson planning, and dedicated nine hours to grading and administrative paper work. An additional nine hours were devoted to seeing individual students, supervising study hall, attending faculty and department meetings, and leading extracurricular activities. She spent another 15 hours working at home during the weekdays and on the weekend grading papers and reading novels and short stories for her courses.

At the secondary school, Wendy coached track and cheerleading. Her principal gave her special praise for developing the cheerleading program at the junior high school. Within a short time, there was so much interest in the program that a new junior varsity squad had to be formed. Wendy made a successful presentation before the school board to get additional funding to add this activity to the extracurricular program.

Her outside interests often related to her coaching. She says, "I am trying to learn soccer so maybe I can coach it. I've expanded my running into track and field and I've learned about some of the field events which I didn't know before." There is another side of Wendy. Recently, she has taken up water coloring both as a way to express herself creatively and to relax.

During the school year, Wendy was assigned a formal mentor who taught at a different grade level and whose classroom was in a different wing of the building. Unfortunately, the mentoring relationship never fully developed. Later in the year, Wendy and a veteran middle school, female English teacher developed a special mentoring relationship that Wendy came to prize. Wendy was also mentored by her department chair and her principal, two men she also had great confidence in as both mentors and supervisors.

FIRST DAY OF TEACHING

In describing her first day of teaching, Wendy emphasizes the need to provide structure and consistency for middle-school-aged students that she taught in her first year. She begins by discussing her first day on the job, then turns to her first day of teaching. Wendy exclaims:

Oh God, it was awful!—my first day on the job. It was very weird because I felt very young. Everyone here is pretty much settled in. I felt like I was a rookie—a greenhorn. The other teachers made jokes about it, too, I'm sure they didn't mean anything by it. My first day actually in the classroom, facing my kids—that was really interesting. I was real nervous about what my kids were going to be like and what kind of students I was going to have. I ended up with some really nice classes so it was kind of a treat. It was nice to have a job, to be getting right back into it. I was hired a week before school started here. So then, to actually have a job and to get back into a classroom and have my own classroom was all very exciting. I wasn't nervous about filling up the time as I was during my actual first day in the classroom, student teaching. Oh, my God!

During each class on the first day, I just said, "I'm a new teacher, so you don't know what I expect of you and I think you should." I set down the ground rules of my classroom in general, how I like my classroom to be run and then what I expect from them as far as work done, their participation, and how grading goes for the semester.

The ground rules—but I think I've lost touch with them, some-what. I wish I had done the same thing all over again at the beginning of the second marking period. Just set up my ground rules again. I think I should have posted them in the room somewhere. I would have had a nice big poster that had my rules instead of just writing them on the board where they're just going to be erased by the next day. I may even do it for the next marking period since I have a new class of kids coming in.

CLASSROOM TEACHING PERSONA

Wendy is a pragmatic and innovative teacher. Her department chair describes her as a "prepared, dedicated, and intelligent" teacher who is "very energetic." She is "always on the move, always moving around and never staying in one place, engaging students with dialogue." Wendy, he reports, has a "natural interest in students—in what they do in her class and outside of her class as well. She's interested in what kind of people they are and the problems and goals they have for themselves." In short, she is a "very person-oriented" teacher. He continues:

> She is also an interesting person to talk with about the field of education, about anything for that matter. Wendy is very active in department meetings. She is not afraid to express her opinions, which sometimes beginning teachers are a little hesitant to do especially around veteran teachers. But she is not apprehensive about that at all. She has some sound opinions, is opinionated, which I like, but she is also quick to see the other point of view.

Her informal mentor, a middle school English teacher, concurs with the department chair. She views Wendy as a "vibrant, committed, and energetic" young teacher who exudes enthusiasm. The mentor states:

> She really is able to motivate kids very readily. She's knowledgeable and she is well-read for someone her age. She's very quick to take in new materials and to develop good lessons from them. I found her to be quite creative with younger kids—a lot of small-group work that involved students actively doing neat things rather than just sitting.

TEACHING APPROACH

In reflecting on what metaphor(s) best capture her teaching style in the classroom, Wendy initially mentioned two roles: police officer and ringmaster. The police officer metaphor, of course, relates to her disciplinary role. "I listen," she states, "to their reasons for why they might be acting that way—like a police officer might listen to why you're speeding and might take it into account. If it's not a good reason, you'll get your ticket. Hopefully, that would cause a student to slow down for a while." Particularly in one ninth-grade class where discipline was a serious problem, she gradually worked out her classroom authority persona in terms of a "cop on the beat" metaphor. She related: "I'm learning to pinpoint the kids who are the problems instead of just blaming the whole group. Now I can catch the problem before it gets out of hand and the kid gets detention." Her department chair indicates that by the end of her first year of teaching, Wendy had mastered this role. "She's always on top of things, always on top of students who are potential discipline problems."

In most classes, however, Wendy's principal role is the ringmaster, which she defines in these terms.

> I try to have all sorts of activities going on in the classroom, and I kind of supervise them. It gets a little "zooey" sometimes, a little crazy, but I guess that's what goes on in my classroom. For example, I do a unit on *The Miracle Worker*. There are lots of different projects that students have to do. I managed to create a miniature version of the set that has all the elements that are described in the first page of the book. So some students might be working on that project. Other groups of students are to memorize and produce a scene from the play. The students can be working on whatever thing they feel is most urgent at the time. My job as ringmaster is to make sure that they are on task, working on something, and to help them if they need help, and to try to direct them.

When informed that her department chair had used the player-coach metaphor to describe her classroom teaching, Wendy agreed that it, too, at times characterizes her teaching style. "I think so because a lot of what I do out on the athletic field comes into my classroom." Asked to detail how that dynamic and more interactive metaphor played itself out in her teaching, Wendy commented:

> I am trying to encourage students to do different things and to really push their experiences out there. I think that's what I try to do in the classroom—get them to look at it and see if they have not overlooked something. I guess that would be where coaching comes in. I don't tell them this is wrong; rather I sort of guide them in that direction. As a coach, I'm not going to say that was no good at all. I'd say this was good but you could do this a little better. You start with the easy tasks and then build up. I start with a short story and deal with aspects

of literature that are accessible to students. It's similar to when you start running; you work on the specifics first and build up from there.

Just as I do in my coaching, in my classroom I don't just say go ahead and do this assignment. I'm out there running. I try to show them. I'm not just telling them to do it. There was an activity we did in the classroom in which they had to pick a feeling word and a color and match that color with that feeling. Rather than just pick a volunteer, I usually do it first. I stand in a circle as part of the group. I don't stand to the side directing. I'm with the group. I usually provide an example. When I ask them to memorize a poem, I memorize one and I go first. I think I use this style of teaching when I ask them to get up in front of the class because that's a big barrier. Also I employ it during conferencing. Students not only have to do conferencing with me but they have to deal with their partner, and I'm an equal on the team. I try to encourage that. What their peers have to say about their paper is just as important as what I have to say. I might be able to pick out more grammar errors, but I try to convince them that I'm not the only expert when it comes to writing.

In describing her teaching style, her department chair provides his perspective.

I think she is a player-coach. Age has a lot to do with that. She's not much older than many of her students. She's a student herself in a sense that she is still learning as we all do. But she is in physical appearance close to the students. In mental activity she is also close to students in that she is a friend as much as a teacher. Yet, there is that distance; they know she is in charge. They can approach her with personal problems; there is a certain rapport with the students. And, as an observer, Wendy led me to see that she was as much a team member as the coach. Like somebody who could play a few games but was still in charge. There is an openness when they approach her, especially with her extracurricular activities—coaching track. I just notice kids coming into her room after school to speak to her.

Wendy's informal mentor supports the department chair's view of her as a player-coach much like a cheerleader coach. She says:

I watched several classes where she was getting students to act out a play. Wendy was totally positive, and encouraging them and jumping up and acting through a scene and saying, "Try this." Then drawing back again and cheering on what they did—encouraging them to put themselves into it. She never held back a minute. She was wide open all the time and they loved that and really responded.

"It really depends on the situation," Wendy indicates as to whether she employs the ringmaster or the player-coach metaphor in her classroom.

> I would say that *The Miracle Worker* is more of a player-coach than the ringmaster unit that I indicated earlier. However, most of the other units are more of the ringmaster. But as I get more comfortable with the unit, and students can do more of their own activities, then I can switch out of the ringmaster role and let them take over.

The conceptual distinctions between the two models center principally on the different degrees of the teacher's participation and role in student learning activities. The ringmaster model, as the term implies, emphasizes the teacher's role as the expert and the authority who gets students to perform both individually and as a team in order to achieve certain pre-scribed learning goals. Under the right conditions, the classroom is a bee-hive of purposeful group- and self-directed activity. The player-coach model emphasizes more the equal participation of teacher and students in meeting learning goals that are also determined by the teacher. When it is working well, the player-coach model, too, promotes productive learning. But it often creates a stronger sense of classroom community and élan than the ringmaster model. Presently, in her teaching, Wendy feels she most often uses the ringmaster role, but would prefer to employ the player-coach model more in her classroom.

While there are important differences between the two models, there is a common core related to the role of the student and the type of learning that should occur during instruction. Both the ringmaster and the player-coach models focus on the student as worker, and both stress student involvement and active as opposed to passive learning in the classroom. These core elements of her working philosophy of classroom teaching are spelled out in detail below. She relates:

> I am trying to make connections, to reach as many kids as I can; to get as many of them interested as I can in what we're doing so that hopefully they get "hooked." Then they'll get the gist of what we're doing. Just get them involved and interested.
>
> Getting kids doing the work is the best thing. Instead of standing up there and writing notes on the board, ask a direct question which they have to answer.
>
> Try to call on different students each time so it's not the "brain" of the class answering all the questions. I even try to encourage those who don't have their hands raised. A lot of times, the ideas are rolling around in their heads but they're just afraid to say it. So I really try to get them involved. For example, I try with eighth graders to give them

a worksheet first because they're not real psyched about having to think on the spot. But if they've been thinking about it by filling in a worksheet or writing in a journal for 10 minutes, then we can discuss the idea. If you just go with it right away, you might have just one student who comes up with the answer. So I plan activities that they can do while writing or while doing something artistically. That gets them working and they might have more fun than just taking notes and answering questions.

Her description of her most successful curriculum unit, which brought out the best in her students, helps illustrate more poignantly the power of this enactive mode of teaching.

I do a creative poetry unit where we not only look at poetry but also create our own poetry. We use a lot of formulas, but I also let students go out on their own and write their own poetry. My best students really come alive here because it really challenges; it is not something they know or have a lot of knowledge about. They really have to challenge themselves because there's no right or wrong. Here's new ground for them; they really have to challenge themselves to be creative and to also exercise their existing knowledge of poetry. They're really good at memorizing a poem but to learn how to add expression and feeling is different and challenging to them. This unit has been successful with lower-level kids—they never thought they could do anything but they do some of the most beautiful poetry. I don't know what it is, maybe not having to use grammar so much.

When asked what were the sources or individuals who encouraged the development of her teaching approach, Wendy indicated that a number of mentors had been very influential. She, of course, cited her college professor, who coincidentally also serves as a role model for her department chair at the Bread Loaf School of English. He, too, indicated that the poet "in the class stimulates thinking to the point of getting people excited about thinking. You just want to keep entering into the dialogue and conversation. He gets more and more out of me." Wendy also cited the cooperating teacher she worked with during her student teaching as an important resource.

My master teacher helped me out with his big emphasis on brainstorming. He would have the whole class brainstorm on the board and then have students do it in their journals. I'm using the method now to get students involved because it gets kids started right on writing. [In the old method] some kids might not even get started. He definitely encouraged me to do such activities.

Other teachers who influenced Wendy were her department chair and several of the eighth-grade English teachers who served as informal mentors to her. In addition, Wendy has attended a number of middle school teacher workshops and taken an athletic coaching course.

Wendy was also asked what knowledge and skills an individual needs to acquire to be good at the kind of student-centered teaching that she does in the middle school. She states:

> Lots of knowledge. Knowledge of the variability of students. More than anything, you need to understand the students and what kinds of different things they're bringing into the classroom. There's no formula for all eighth-grade students, especially eighth-grade students. They all come in with their different perks. Every student is different, every student needs to be treated differently.
>
> Second, subject matter—I would say—not just reading the book once but reading it the second time, slowly, with the kids makes a world of difference in the curriculum. And being flexible with the curriculum, for example, trying different ways of teaching grammar. You can just sit there with the grammar book, but I think the new trend is going to applied grammar. The more they write the more they use grammar, then they start to catch on, hopefully, get it.
>
> I also feel strongly about sharing. That means not being afraid to ask other teachers for help when you need it, and also if you find something good pass it on. That's a valuable source.
>
> There are, of course, communication skills—being able to communicate at the times when you need to. There are two levels of communication—the teaching level and the interpersonal level. There are also discipline or classroom management skills that are important.

As a follow-up to the first part of her answer, Wendy was also asked whether it is necessary for her in the classroom to take into account student differences in terms of gender, race, or social class. Her comments illustrate her democratic, equalitarian classroom ethic. She views her students as individuals whom she treats differently only in terms of their academic performance and effort. When teaching she wishes to treat all students fairly, compassionately, and with their best interest in mind. She wants them to succeed, not fail, and to do so in a "safestop" environment. Wendy states:

> I don't look at it as their race or gender. For instance, I don't look at boys and girls as different. I look at personalities. There are wild girls and wild boys. I don't see a pattern in gender. The most I change my

teaching is when I look at their work. I look at what they've produced and what they're capable of as students. When I see a kid who never before wrote a complete sentence and all of a sudden the student puts together a final product of four pages, I take that into account over a student who always writes perfect grammar and gets things all together. With the final product, I ask isn't this more than this student ever produced? Or, boy, this paper really stinks compared to the A+ from before.

Even within cliques there are definitely some kids who make comments; and I try to discourage that by saying, "How would you like it if someone said something bad about you?" Treat it that way. I try not to make it obvious that I would treat them any differently.

I don't make a habit of calling on kids whose hands are not raised. If they look like they are confused about a question, I'm not going to embarrass them or not so much embarrass them but set them up for failure.

If I know that a kid is thinking about a question and might have a solution, then I may call on him or her. That's why I have them do the worksheets. By going around and checking the worksheets, I have a good idea of which ones they've answered. So they're the ones I go for. I start by giving them some success.

EVALUATION

In describing her strengths and weaknesses as a classroom teacher, Wendy reflects:

I don't know how I got it or where I got it but I just have some sort of connection with eighth graders. I find that I understand this level better than ninth graders. I don't know why that is, maybe it's just because I've been working with them more or because they are nicer. One of my biggest strengths is my commitment. I always want to keep trying to do something better. I want to know more about how I can do this better. I also think teaching is more than an 8:00 a.m. to 3:00 p.m. job. If you don't have that commitment—without that commitment—you're not going to get to know those students as well. Other things count, too, such as coaching. I feel strongly about how I've gotten to know students through coaching, and how that's helped to give me some insights into the classroom. For instance, I had the opportunity to coach junior high cheerleading this year—the shyest, quietest girl in my classes came out in cheerleading and I never knew she had that side of her.

I still feel I need to improve in learning to understand students. I can think of specific cases where I was a little bit hard on them, and I forgot to give them the opportunity to tell me why they were acting that way. I might just send a kid out of the room who was misbehaving and then forget to follow up and say, "Why were you doing that? Can we avoid it next time?" Another thing I need to work on, too, is my attitude with students who are always causing me to have to speak to them. My patience is shorter with them. It's easy to jump on those persons, you're always jumping on them for doing something.

I also need to read more. I need to read books that are philosophical discussions. I need to find the time and energy for it—the type of books you read in college.

In responding to "What is your main worry as a teacher?" Wendy reflects on her chosen vocation.

In the future, I worry that I'm not doing a good job teaching—that I'm not getting my students interested and yet I still teach. That I'll be one of those teachers who's burned out. I also worry about a student changing so much and being affected in the junior high year in a way that I could possibly ruin somebody's life by something I say. I think that is a realistic worry—that as a teacher you say something that makes them crawl into their little shell. I don't think I have done that yet, but it is always a concern that you could burn out the candle for English or for school.

Wendy rated her first year as successful. Moreover, her department chair, her informal mentor, and her principal rate her as an excellent beginning teacher. She is considered one of the best first-year teachers in the school. In fact, the principal ranks her as one of the two best young teachers he has seen in his seven-year tenure at the secondary school, which has seen an influx of new teachers in recent years because of retirements. Her informal mentor ranks her as "outstanding" and provides this assessment of Wendy as a teacher.

I had parents come in to see me who had twin sons, very bright students. One was in my class and the other in Wendy's. The parents were thrilled to death with the English instruction their kids were getting and felt both boys were doing well. They felt good about me, they felt good about her. Very high praise for a first-year teacher.

In her first year, Wendy says her toughest problems were "setting my limits with discipline" and not having enough time to prepare properly.

"When I was running a unit, I'd try to read the book over the weekend, then as I did the unit I would reread it again. I was exhausted from doing these things." At the end of the first year, she listed these four things she would try to do differently in her next year of teaching.

1. Have everything prepared for a whole unit in advance.
2. Set down my rules and expectations and stick to them from the beginning of the semester.
3. Try to get to know my students even sooner.
4. Look for innovative ideas throughout the summer.

POSTSCRIPT

Comparing her first year to her second year of teaching during a follow-up interview in the summer of 1990, she concluded:

> I would say I learned a lot during my first year that I applied my second year. But in trying to budget my time better, I overlooked some things in the second year. Sometimes I'd be doing something that would save time in teaching, but I could have been doing something else that would help my students. Instead of correcting tests when some students finished, I could have figured out something creative to do with the early finishers. That's not a great example, but I got caught up in some things and forgot about student activities. The year before I was constantly thinking about that. I feel better this year in that I feel more confident as a teacher, but some of that energy that I had the first year, maybe I lost a bit—not altogether certainly, but a bit.

Both during her first- and second-year teaching, Wendy was "riffed" (reduction in teaching force). While hired back by the end of her first year of teaching, she was let go after her second year because of a decline in student enrollment at her secondary school. She is now teaching in another northern New England middle school.

CHAPTER 3

Teacher as Jazz Musician: James Crawford-Williams

James Crawford-Williams, a 25-year-old African-American, was born in Pittsburgh, Pennsylvania. He is referred to by his students and some members of the faculty as CW. At the age of 8, he and his family moved to Oberlin, Ohio. His father was a postal carrier until his early retirement because of health problems. For the past 12 years, his mother has been a Head Start teacher. Both parents were initially "not enthusiastic" about his desire to teach. They preferred that he choose a profession such as law that would "establish him financially." He indicates that they now understand how his vocation "sustains" him and are supportive of his decision. He has one sister, who lives in Atlanta, Georgia. He has been married slightly over a year. His wife recently completed a master's degree in child psychology at Harvard School of Education.

As an undergraduate, CW attended Yale University where he majored in philosophy. In 1989, he earned a master's degree in theology from Harvard Divinity School. While he did not complete a teacher licensure program, he did take some education courses at Yale as an undergraduate and several others at Harvard School of Education when doing graduate work at the university. He presently teaches in a public secondary school in Massachusetts. His teaching license is pending.

CW decided on teaching, as he says:

Probably when I got the job. Yet, I came to that decision loosely when I was in junior high school. When I came to the summer school program at Phillips Academy in Andover in my ninth-grade year, I was exposed to the more comforting college-level seminar style of teaching, which really forged a deep impression on me. I really thought that was a great thing to experience—good teaching. From then on, I knew that I wanted to teach on some level. The question as I got into college was how to go about the more practical dimensions of learning to teach—how to study to be a good teacher. At that point,

I became uncertain because I noticed that requirements for teacher prep and stuff like that didn't interest me. I felt that actually studying how to teach would put me under some parameters and constraints that I didn't want.

I dealt with teaching in a different way—as a minister. I went to Harvard Divinity School to sort out my calling and came to terms with this sort of teaching ministry that I call it now. After graduate school, there was nothing else that I wanted to do.

His reasons for teaching are multifaceted. CW is attracted to the profession because he feels he has "some skills that lend themselves well to teaching" and because of the nine-month academic schedule and the more flexible working hours. However, the major attraction relates to the vocational role itself. He states:

I began to understand the power that one actually exerts in the role of the teacher. This whole notion of forming and shaping and molding young people's consciousness is very appealing to me. Not saying I want to mold it to be like my own, but I just want to help students form their consciousness in an open way. There's not another forum that exists for that potential effect.

During his academic career, CW had role models who influenced his decision to teach and to develop a clear perspective on the nature of teaching. In Oberlin, Ohio, two sixth-grade teachers, a woman and an African-American who was the only black male teacher he was to have until college were "very formative." A high school teacher who was an Oberlin College graduate and who CW thought "very creative" was another important educator in his life. However, the individual who was to have the greatest effect on CW was an African-American professor at Yale Divinity School during his undergraduate years. CW relates:

What he did for me was really threefold. On one hand, he showed me that the life of the mind could be liberating. Second, he showed me that I could actually be a part of the academy without being co-opted by its values and its way of life. I could hold on to what was essentially me and really exist in the academic world as a teacher/professor. Third, I think his presentation, his interpersonal skills, his pedagogical understanding have just opened me up to a whole new light. He has one of the most refined minds in this country today. He held his students as equals. He would ask critical questions and be willing to entertain dialogue. It was a dialogical process of teaching that was not teacher-centered. Probably the most formative experience in my own understanding of teaching came from him.

The public school in which CW teaches is a Grade 9–12 very competitive secondary school in one of Boston's nearby wealthier suburban cities. Over 90% of the school's 1,100 students go on to higher education. While most of the students are white, 5% of the student population is African-American. Asian-Americans and Hispanics make up another 2% of the enrollment. The school itself has often been ranked as one of the finest in the country. CW taught five courses and had three daily preparations: ninth-grade world history, eleventh-grade U.S. history, and twelfth-grade psychology (first semester) and social psychology (second semester). His total student load was roughly 100 students. He characterizes the general atmosphere of his school as "loose."

An experienced African-American social studies teacher was assigned to CW as a mentor. The buddy teacher was helpful in providing practical advice on how the school operates. A female social studies teacher who serves as department chair was also a significant mentor for CW in providing curricular advice and emotional support. The school principal also offered support to him during the academic year.

FIRST DAY OF TEACHING

Like other first-year teachers, CW speaks of his first day of teaching as one of anxiety and exhilaration.

> I was nervous, of course. I had done substitute work before, but this was like the real show. I think my anxiety was evident, although students couldn't detect it because they were as nervous as I was. Actually, it went very well, very well. I had planned out some games which the kids were really into. It was such a well-planned day for me. I had planned everything for the first few days so it went well.
>
> On the first day, I tried to stay away from talking about classroom rules. I try to downplay the authority. What I do is pass out a course description on the first day, then I try to just dive right into it and make them think, wow, this is going to be hard for me—fun but rough. I try to hit them hard the first day, set the tone that this is going to be serious academic inquiry. You always want to start off a little more strict than you are so you can loosen up. If you start too loose, you can't tighten up.

CLASSROOM TEACHING PERSONA

As a teacher, CW is described by his principal as "charismatic, out-going, and well-adjusted" and by his department chair as "enthusiastic, bright, and caring." His mentor states, "He's energetic, provocative, and understanding." CW himself believes that the following personal qualities he possesses fit well with teaching: "my natural skills in making people comfortable, being sensitive to where people are, and being able to interact and stimulate dialogue." His department chair comments:

> His sense of caring about kids and their learning comes through right away. Students know that he has expectations for them and he wants them to fulfill them. It's typical of him to start a class commenting on work that they've done which he may have just graded or is in the process of reading or anticipates giving them. The kinds of things he says to them about their work in general just makes it clear to them that he regards what they are doing as important, that he expects them to work hard. When he gets into the subject matter, it's also clear that he really cares about what he is teaching them—that what he is teaching them is important for them to know. He uses a variety of strategies that help get them involved in what they're doing. It's fun as well as meaningful.

His official mentor observes that

> CW is a person who has very high standards, particularly in terms of himself and what his character is. Part of it is his divinity background, I'm sure. Yet, he is willing to understand and appreciate and deal with the shortcomings of others. He does that in an effective way. He not only is able to see what is on the surface, but is able to peer beneath the veneer.
>
> He's also suffused with energy, and that is a wonderful combination. He can listen to students endlessly and work with them to resolve their problems in school and out of school. I've just seen him work with so many students so often, and just about everything he'd do was on the mark.
>
> When a student criticizes him, he doesn't take it personally. I've never seen him yell at anybody. I've never seen him blow up, yet he commands respect in a very clear way from students and faculty alike, and he isn't real pushy. He has things that he believes in but he doesn't come in and dump them on somebody. But he will stand up for what he thinks is right. He enjoys the academic debate tremendously and

is willing to participate in it. As seriously as he takes himself, he understands his weaknesses, and I think strives to correct them. I think those are tremendous strengths.

Besides his high school teaching, CW also taught a course twice a week on African-American theology at a Boston-area college. During the school year, he served as a faculty advisor to the Black Student Union and coached ninth-grade girls' basketball. These extracurricular activities helped him establish better rapport with students. "I get to see the kids," he said, "outside of the classroom and they get to see me outside of the classroom, too. It helps establish our connections as humans." For recreation, he plays basketball and also completes a daily regimen of physical exercise. In reflecting on his life and commitments, particularly outside of school, he comments:

> I immerse myself in trying to give those who are dehumanized, demoralized, a voice. This I try to do in my teaching. But outside of the school, I'm a lay minister. I do some preaching and some writing also. I try to allow suffering to speak, to make victims visible to those with power so they can understand the situation, the context of people who are oppressed. I generally do that in relation to the community that I feel most accountable to, which is the African-American community. I do it mostly by writing and teaching.
>
> I am certainly a progressive, a left theologian who understands God in terms of liberating the oppressed. I adhere to and practice a social gospel that is probably an amalgamation of not only Christianity, Islam, and a number of other Western traditions but includes some Eastern ones as well. So my understanding of religion is just an understanding of the spirit. I do consider myself to be a prophetic Christian, which means that I candidly confront the tragic character of human history, but don't allow the immensity of what is to take away from the vastness of what may be.

In sum, CW conceives of his teaching as a sacred calling—a teaching ministry in the public schools that attempts to fuse key elements of both the vocation of the ministry and profession of teaching. The late Perry Miller (1964), the distinguished American colonial historian, referred to the Puritans' arrival in New England as an "errand in the wilderness"—a mission to serve, as John Winthrop said, as a "City Upon the Hill" (p. 2). It seems that CW, too, has a similar task in modern American secular society. In the following sections the dynamic and evolving dimensions of the teaching mission are defined.

TEACHING APPROACH

In reflecting on what metaphor he would use to describe his role in the classroom, CW responded:

> I like to use the musical metaphor. I like classical jazz, and in that tradition, it's how the ensemble moves with one another. In the class-room, I try not to consider myself a leader. I try to stress the fact I'm on equal ground with the students, but I've had a little more experi-ence than they have. I'm here to share that but I also want to share their experiences. So that establishes this notion of the ensemble creating music in everyone. Again, ideally everyone is contributing and moving together—like a jazz music composition.
>
> This is a metaphor for the teacher and students being in the process of discovering together. The presupposition is that we be-come open, ready for anything. We are always in the mode of creating some sort of textuality because we are all intertwined in this move-ment. More practically, it is like a discussion of a topic that gains momentum and gains definition by all of us participating in dialogue in creating it.
>
> For instance, one activity that illustrates the metaphor-in-action, and worked pretty well for my ninth graders in world history, was a chapter in the history text that dealt with the crusades. What I did one day in class was have them come up with a rhyme for two words that were connected with the crusades that they didn't know the definitions for. One could be Peter the Hermit or Richard the Lion-hearted. It took a while but they all did it. Then we went around the room and sang the whole rhyme that turned out to be like a rap, and we enjoyed that. I found that the best students in the class felt like they were learning and learned what the words were and remembered them.

His department chair provides another example of this classical jazz mode of teaching. She relates:

> A ninth-grade class had done a reading assignment and had a number of terms that they were supposed to have written out definitions for. Rather than just collecting the definitions or just going over them, what he did was to list them on the board in a predetermined order and ask the first student to give the definition and use the word in a sentence. Then the second student had to repeat what the first student had said, and then define and use the second term on the board in a sentence, and so forth. The anticipated outcome was that in the end

they would have used all of the words in what everybody else had said in a kind of story. The way in which it was done was particularly effective. If a kid was hesitant, he would ask a question or provide leading information until the kid finally got to the point of saying something meaningful. The repetition was encouraging them to practice what they had heard and to do the job well. The kids felt like they were in this together—they became supportive of each other in the process, and they went through an activity where they all came out having practiced the skill that he was getting at.

The further elaborations of his department chair highlight other features of his classroom teaching that focus on his personal qualities as a teacher and on his instructional goals. She states:

He is somebody who cares about the outcome, the winning of the sport or the learning of the material, but also who realizes that there is a lot to the process of getting kids to work together or getting kids to work individually—that there are a lot of intellectual skills that kids need to learn—that they won't learn as quickly as they might— that they won't practice them as consistently as they should—but that the effort of the teacher has always got to be consistent in working toward those things.

In the classroom, he's always a presence and he always controls what goes on in the classroom, but there's a lot of involvement of the kids. Sometimes the involvement is intended to let them have a good time and to let them achieve things—classes in psychology and U.S. history where the kids get very much involved in the subject through debate over the issues. He encourages the students to talk to each other, not just to him. He creates a classroom atmosphere where they are willing to test their ideas and to try to see issues from other perspectives. I think he fosters that kind of individual reflection and active participation that you want to see with kids.

In fact, when CW was asked what he was really trying to achieve as a teacher in the classroom, he responded by emphasizing the development of the critical perspective and a sense of personal hope and efficacy in students. Here is what he said.

I want to raise critical consciousness. Again, this notion of allowing suffering to be visible is of primary importance to me. I'm trying to get them to understand that the underlying issue related to Harvey Milk's death in the film that we discussed today is bigger than Dan White having pressure from his kids. This is an issue where

White has killed two men in cold blood, not primarily because he's homophobic but essentially because mainstream culture has dictated that this is appropriate behavior, and allowed him to get away with it.

So I want them to be creative thinkers and do some analysis of whatever we see or talk about. I'm trying to help them to come to self-understanding—connect this now to your own life. That's why I said in class that students didn't link it enough to personal experience. So I want to help form self-understanding, how to look at themselves on these issues.

Finally, I truly try to instill them with a sense of love and hopefulness. I work on how I relate to them, it's good to see them, how I love the class, how I'm glad everybody dropped in. Handshakes, hugs, personal contact. This notion of hope, I try to infuse that in materials, in my own presentations. Being hopeful in spite of everything today that looks hopeless. That we're going against the odds here, that's okay because I try to inoculate them with this notion of hope and that links to transformation on a social level. They are certainly not mainstream values but I think they're worthy.

CW discussed what knowledge and skills it takes to do this kind of teaching.

Knowledge for freedom. Knowledge that helps one interpret, describe, and evaluate one's own situation. This is why ideological discussion has to take place, whether it's in a history class or psychology class. Going away from the course with a better understanding of not only how things work around you, but how things are for you, is primary. Knowledge that a person who is committed and dedicated can make a change—not only personal change but also social and political change.

I think you need skills that none of us probably possesses. You need intellectual skills, social skills, and, if you want to be a teacher, skills in dealing with institutional structure. (I don't have those skills, I don't want them, and I wish no one had to have them.) You also need, of course, to be able to relate to people—be sensitive.

We need sensitive, dedicated men and women in trying to enhance the critical powers of the young and help dedicate them to the values of the intellect. What distresses me is that I see a number of teachers who are only interested in bringing home a paycheck. I couldn't fathom doing anything just for that purpose.

COUNSELING MISSION

His mentor calls CW a "religious pilgrim who happens to be a teacher. He's like the pilgrim who drops in at an inn in the wintertime and helps all the people, particularly those who are a little down." He relates how CW plays out this role in his hectic daily schedule.

He was involved in so much. He was very active in the Black Student Union, in the black achievement task force, the girls' junior varsity basketball. He was active in the athletic booster association. He participated in their special night and drew the greatest applause and helped them raise most of the money. All the various things he did were unbelievable. He just seems to be almost ubiquitous in terms of helping solve problems in problem areas. Anybody can go and head something, particularly when they're getting paid. But, you see, a lot of stuff he did—hard stuff—he got no money for. It wasn't particularly a status thing to do, and there were a lot of risks involved. I think he did it because it was the right thing to do—somebody asked. Somebody at the inn needed help, and there he was. It was done with a lot of energy and a lot of time. Those after-school meetings, then you go coach. One of those trips on the road, then you get home at 7:00, 8:00, or 9:00 p.m. at night. For a person with three different class preparations, that's not easy. All new students. My God! Right?

CW was particularly effective with many of the difficult-to-reach students that he had in his classes. His mentor reported:

He succeeded with kids this year that other people couldn't handle last year and the year before. He did very well with them. I know that because I was across the hall from him, and I handled those kids years before and I also know the teachers who had them immediately before he did. A couple of those students were tough people to deal with. Their whole program was disruption and negativity.

According to his mentor, two reasons help explain his success with these difficult-to-reach students.

He's a good motivator. He motivates people well, not in a la-la type thing, but he gets people to ask the question, "Am I operating at a high level, or am I just moving?" And he does that without beating them over the head. "If you're going to come to class, you might as well do the work here," CW would say. And most of them seem to buy that. He is also very good at saying positive things to people, and with no strings attached—"It's real good." But he doesn't couple it with if's, and's, and but's. It's just a flat-out compliment. In this society, we don't do that very well. It is a major weakness at this school. Around here, everybody—teachers and students alike—feel, "Well, what else do they want me to do?" He's not that way. He'll look at something and say, "This is a winner." The kids feel pretty good about that.

A second reason for his success with the troubled students is, of course, his willingness to listen to them and counsel them. Again, his mentor relates, "When students come into his class and they've got some problems that are interfering with schoolwork, they will come to him and say they have a problem. And he will say, 'Well, let's try to get this problem solved, then you can deal with what we have to deal with here.'"

CW provided pastoral help to many of these students during the academic year. Below he discusses two such cases.

I was able to connect with students; students are able to confide in me and that's part of what I want to be doing. I had a student who was going through an abortion who told no one else but me and we got together with her mother, to get her to voice her concerns.

Also I was able to push another student who was an African-American female who had such potential—I couldn't believe it—but she just did nothing. I sat her down one day and said, "Look you have such potential!" I made a deal with her. I said, "If you come to my class every day on time, do all the homework, and work hard on tests, then I will give you a passing grade." The first term she had flunked and I was forced to give her an F. I said, "If you make this deal with me, I will give you a D instead of an F for the term."

She didn't take it. She said she couldn't come to class on time and do all her homework. I stayed on her for two days and said, "Look, this is ridiculous—I'm really going out of my way to try to come to terms with you on how we can improve your time here, why don't you want to take me up on it?"

One day, she broke down and started crying and said she couldn't do it. Then I realized that she had no confidence. So that night she called me and said she would make a deal. The other side of the deal was that if she missed class, then she would get an F for the second term. It was a harsh deal, but I thought it was worth it to give it a try. So I gave her the D for the first term on the basis that she would start coming on time, with the work done, and do all the tests, etc. She called me and said she would do it, and she began to transform before my very eyes and ended up getting A's every term thereafter. She got the highest grade in the class for two terms.

EVALUATION

CW rates his first year of teaching as very successful. Reflecting on the experience, he relates:

> I got a letter the last day of school that made me cry, and it said everything I ever wanted to do this whole year. One student, a male Hispanic, told me everything that I had done, everything I dreamed of doing as a teacher, that I had done! A number of things—that he loved the course, the way I taught it. He felt he learned more about life from the course, that I was easy to relate to and accessible. He felt that I was an incredible intellect, and that I was inspiring in terms of pushing students to be involved in a number of issues, socially. He was going to use me as a paragon, and he actually said that he's thinking of becoming a teacher now, which makes me feel so good. I can't describe it.

However, CW is self-critical about his teaching. He feels he needs to improve his instruction by "coming up with better methods for my style of teaching." He comments:

> Why I can't do that seems to be because I'm really resisting what people tell me. I don't want to taint the teacher–student relationship with something contrived. I want to be so real that I don't want to think about it. I know that's like saying, "I want to write poetry but I'll never read other poets because I don't want to write like them." I need to talk with an associate and watch other teachers do their thing— although initially I'm very resistant to that. Once I realize they aren't trying to impose how they do things on me, then I'm good at adapting it.

He continues his self-assessment.

> Another problem is that I need to give a little more structure to allow students to be clear as to what happens in each class. "Why did we do that?" I'm pretty weak on the board, too. I don't like to write on the board at all. Maybe I'm just kind of lazy but I just don't like to put stuff on the board. When I look at it after everybody's gone, I just say, "Why is it there?" There is no systematic presentation that is visible

when I use the board, so I need to work on it. See, that makes me
mad but it makes me feel good, too, because I don't want it to be very
systematic. I don't want to be dogmatic in a presentation. So I'm
happy when I look at the board and it seems chaos—but I wonder, "Is
it like this in their minds, too?" Or, is there some clear thread?

His department chair, too, feels there is some room for improvement
in his teaching. In particular, she says, he needs to improve his pacing—
"getting from here to there in his survey courses." She remarks that CW
would often get behind in these courses because he wanted his students to
understand and not simply learn the "facts." Thus he needs to improve in
making conscious decisions not only about what to include but what to
exclude in a survey course. "That's a problem," she states, "which will never
be easily or even ever overcome. A lot of experienced teachers have that
problem, too." She concludes, "Obviously, there are things he will do better
as he goes along, but I've been continually impressed by his sense of understanding kids and understanding how they learn and trying consciously to
plan things that will help them to be engaged in what's important."

His supervisors and mentor rate him as "excellent," "in the top category," "one of the best young teachers" in the school. As one of them
commented, "He has a natural sense of teaching—he's rather unusual."
Another responded, "In terms of insight, knowledge base, and experiential
base, there's really no comparison."

As a teacher, CW would like to have the reputation as a "critically
intellectual, creative, and engaged person not only in teaching but in life
itself. I'd like to be known as a long-distance runner in the struggle for
justice, and I'd like my students to know that I'm morally committed—not
a professor of one thing and a doer of another."

Finally, as a social activist, CW fervently believes that school must
change in order to meet the needs of students and to empower both teachers
and the students they serve. He concludes:

I wonder how the educational system can be transformed. It subordi-
nates teachers to an unrealistic pace and enormity of tasks which do
not allow them to be the transformative intellectuals they need to be.
Teachers should be free men and women with a special dedication to
enhancing the critical powers and creative energies of the young. But
we almost can't be because of the constraints we're under.

Also students are far too often subordinated to the authority of
teachers and to grades. This ends up producing misconstrued values.
Teachers, administrators, and the system, however, wind up actually
responsible for this situation. The system is not true to the meaning
of education, which should not be to give one the skills and abilities

to take a secure place in democratic society, but to transform society so that it meets the collective needs of the individuals of which it is comprised.

POSTSCRIPT

In both his first and second year of teaching, CW was "riffed" from his teaching position, only to be rehired by the end of each of the academic years. However, during his third year of teaching, he will be part time in social studies and part time as a counselor in the Black Achievement Program that was initiated by the school several years ago. He continues to teach courses in the African-American religious experience at a nearby university.

CHAPTER 4

Teacher as Song Leader: Elizabeth Alberto

Elizabeth Alberto grew up in Andover, Massachusetts, where she attended the local public schools. She graduated from high school second in her class. Both of Elizabeth's parents were supportive of her decision to teach, particularly her mother, who was at one time a high school teacher. She has an older sister and two younger brothers, one of whom may become a music teacher.

A very bright and hard-working student, Elizabeth graduated *summa cum laude* from Middlebury College in 1987. She majored in Spanish and had a minor concentration in teacher education. She student-taught Spanish at both the junior and senior high school levels at the local Grade 7–12 secondary school in Middlebury. At the end of her junior year, she was elected to the Phi Beta Kappa Society.

After completing college, she married a Spanish national she met while studying abroad during her junior year. For the first year after college they resided in Madrid, where she taught English as a second language. Each summer Elizabeth and her husband visit their family in Spain. These experiences have helped her develop near-native competence in the language and have provided her with unique insights and firsthand knowledge of the Spanish culture. She now teaches Spanish at the same wealthy Boston suburban high school where James Crawford-Williams teaches.

Elizabeth's interest in teaching developed during her high school years when she was a camp counselor. By the end of her sophomore year in college, she had made a commitment to teach. Elizabeth had no one role model who influenced her teaching style. As she says, "I had as my role model a combination of all the teachers I had in school. There's no one specific person, although I did have in my first two years of Spanish a very good teacher, and I learned a lot from him. He provided a good foundation for the language and how to teach it. I worked with it from there."

In her first year at the 1,100-student suburban high school, Elizabeth taught four classes and had a number of supervisory duties such as hall monitoring, which was the equivalent of a fifth course. She had a total of 85 students, including many tenth graders and some ninth and eleventh graders who were starting Spanish I. Unlike CW, she describes the highly competitive school's atmosphere as "moderately strict" rather than "loose." These different characterizations by the two beginners are perhaps because of their varying perspectives and school experiences, and the decentralized nature of the school's power and authority. The school is operated on the house system, and each of the three houses is led by a headmaster and faculty who may establish norms and disciplinary practices for their administrative unit that are somewhat different from those of the other units. Because Elizabeth and CW teach in separate houses on the suburban school campus, it is understandable that they perceive the school atmosphere somewhat differently.

During her first year of teaching, Elizabeth worked close to a 60-hour week. Of this work week, more than 40 hours were spent at the school teaching, preparing lessons, and grading papers. Five additional hours weekly were spent working with individual students. Elizabeth also spent 15 hours at home on weekdays and weekends correcting papers and preparing her daily lessons. During the school year, Elizabeth was involved in a number of extracurricular activities. She states, "I have chaperoned many activities—dances, music concerts, and helped organize barbecues, etc." Finally, during her initial year at the high school, Elizabeth led a Costa Rican exchange during the spring vacation. All of these activities, she believes, "help to improve my relationship with the students because they see that I like to spend time with them outside of class. In other words, I don't just teach my class and go home!"

During the academic year, Elizabeth developed a very close relationship with an experienced, female Spanish teacher who came to serve as her informal mentor. This veteran teacher provided her with both practical suggestions and emotional support. Elizabeth's department chair, a female French teacher, was also a colleague that she often confided in about her teaching beyond the normal supervisory visits and conferences. The school principal, too, was helpful to Elizabeth in promoting emotional support throughout the academic year.

FIRST DAY OF TEACHING

Like other beginners, Elizabeth describes her first day of teaching as one of high anxiety and of setting down the ground rules to her students. She relates:

I was very nervous. I was very stern. Basically, I just read them the rules. The first day of class was a shortened period of 30 minutes in order to get all of the rotating blocks in. This was enough time to pass out books, do book slips, and have them write out index cards for me with their names and phone numbers.

Basically, I told them what I expected of the class. I told them the first and foremost rule in my class is that you will respect whomever is speaking at the moment. You will be considerate of everyone else in the class. If I ever see the slightest glimmer of someone telling someone else to shut up or that's a stupid answer, we'll stop everything right there. I don't ever want to hear that. This does not happen in this classroom. But I was nervous!

CLASSROOM TEACHING PERSONA

Elizabeth is a structured and caring teacher. Her principal states that "she's bright and able, hard-working and highly idealistic. Really she is a lovely person in every way. She's a kind of sweet-looking person, quiet in some ways, but she's surprisingly tough-minded." Her informal mentor states that "she is one of the finest people you've ever met. Strong as far as her moral fiber is concerned, strong as far as her beliefs are concerned, and strong as far as what she does in her classroom. Elizabeth is one of the most giving people that I have ever had the pleasure to work with."

Elizabeth's department chair elaborates on the personal traits that make her an unusually successful beginning teacher at her suburban school.

From the first time I interviewed her, Elizabeth appeared to have a good sense of herself, who she was, what she wanted to do, and a realistic sense of her accomplishments. I never felt she was arrogant or big-headed, but that she knew that she was good in her field. On the other hand, she has a softness about her that is appealing in dealing with high school students. She has a kind of humane view of students and their needs, while not going over the edge of what I've sometimes seen in teachers—of them thinking they're going to cure all ills and solve all their students' problems, and be friends and mother and all that. She values and understands that her main goal is to teach students Spanish, first and foremost, and secondarily to help them in any way to grow as human beings.

She also reads all her memos, she keeps up-to-date with what's happening in the school, and she handled a very difficult homeroom. It's interesting in this culture, if you can't handle your homeroom, then you can't win the respect of your colleagues no matter how intelligent you are. She inherited a very difficult bunch of kids who had been allowed to do too much, get away with too much. In no time at all, they were all "standing and saluting," which is not easy for someone like Elizabeth. She looks like she's 12 years old, but it doesn't take long for anybody—adults and youngsters—to realize that she's someone to be reckoned with.

The other side of Elizabeth is that she is not afraid in spite of her exterior, her demeanor of being extremely competent, to come to my office and sit down and say, "I'm having trouble in this area, what do you think I should do?" or "I expect you will be getting a phone call from a parent, here's the story." So she has inner strength but enough sense to know that sometimes she needs help.

Her department chair also indicates that Elizabeth has a significant impact on her department in terms of providing greater collegiality and intellectual leadership to its other faculty members. The department chair elaborates:

At department meetings she always listens carefully and she is polite. Her body language is attentive even to members of the department who may be saying things that take a long time and may not be saying too much. She waits, and when she's ready to make her statements, she makes them and she's always on target. Without being aggressive, she manages to get her points across. She won the respect of all of her colleagues in the school who have dealt with her almost immediately, not because she's so competent in Spanish and not because she's so competent as a teacher, but because she handles everything with such sensitivity and sensibleness.

Because of the way she operates—which is quietly but effectively—she has raised the whole tenor of expectations in the department. We have some very fine faculty in Spanish, but I would speculate they don't see their group self-image as intellectuals but rather as "people people." Because of what Elizabeth has brought to the school: the knowledge about how to use computers, her knowledge of foreign language oral proficiency, her knowledge of Spanish film and Spanish authors, she has kind of lifted everybody up and helped her colleagues see themselves in a little bit different light and to improve professionally.

TEACHING APPROACH

As a reserved and modest young adult, Elizabeth speaks concisely and matter-of-factly about herself as a teacher. But like a Hemingway short story, her words convey but the tip of the iceberg about her classroom teaching. In many ways, her working philosophy can be summed up in the old adage, "Actions speak louder than words." Perhaps the Taoist philosopher Lao-Tzu's (1963) view of leadership captures her classroom teaching style best. "As for the best leaders, the people do not notice their existence. . . . When the best leaders' work is done, the people say we did it ourselves" (p. 5). Her mentors' voices help fill out and reveal the dynamics of her teaching perspective and of her élan and the ambience in her classroom.

Elizabeth states that her classroom teaching metaphor is that of a "song leader"—part coach, part facilitator, and part team member. It is an interactive, cooperative style of teaching that requires oral participation and active involvement of her students. She explains:

> I guide them through the tune, and they join in with me—without them, there is no song. Within the bounds of the tune, they have the opportunity to change, add, or take away from, however they see fit. For example, I may teach the structure of commands. Together, we discuss when such a structure would be used; then they, in small groups, make up a skit to demonstrate its use.
>
> The picture I get in my mind of my teaching is someone who is in the middle of a circle, in the middle of a group of kids—not in the front telling them what to do, but in the middle and helping them learn their part and play their role.
>
> In fact, I do keep students in a circle. I don't have them in rows. In the circle there might be smaller circles—a group of students with a skit to write or something to read and report back to the class about by the end of the period. I would go from group to group making sure they're on the right track and answering questions.
>
> Also, whatever I ask them to do, I'll do myself. I never ask them to do something that I wouldn't do. If, for example, I ask them to do a skit where they have to ask their mother for permission to go out, then many times I will do a skit with one of the groups—I'll join in either because there's an odd number or just to be one of the group. One time as a first activity, I asked them to do a bumper sticker that describes each of them and then explain it to the class. I started off the group by explaining mine to break the ice and to show it was okay to say something that maybe you might not have wanted to say.

Her department chair elaborates on this type of classroom teaching that emphasizes student performance, initiative, and responsibility.

> There was one class that I observed in which she brought in a vase, an odd-looking vase—a garage-sale vase. Her students had just fin- ished the previous week buying and selling and exchanging money,

etc. When she brought in the vase, she said to the students, "This is a rare art object." (She said it all in Spanish, and it was wonderful.) Of course, that was funny because it was really a sad-looking vase. Then she said, "I'm going to ask two of you to work together. I want one of you to sell the vase, and another of you to be the buyer. I don't want this to be an easy sale. I want to see a little bartering going on here." I thought this was going to be interesting because in one sense, the students hadn't prepared for this learning task. It could be a nerve-wracking experience, but the fact that she first of all toned it all down by taking this not-too-beautiful vase and making it into an elaborate art object made the tenor of the class relaxed. She's very sensitive not to jump in right away when they stop talking—when they were looking for words. But she knew when the conversation needed a little push, and she might say, for example, "Your price is too low, jack it up." In fact, by just knowing when to come in and give that little assistance, she helped students get along and carry on their conversation, which was her goal. She didn't leave them out there in the cold; she made it relaxed, and they knew that. They also knew that she wasn't going to give them everything, every time they got stuck. You could tell from the way they were groping for words and how they were trying to be clever and use expressions they had learned.

Her informal mentor's comments reveal other aspects of her song-leader style, which emphasizes cooperative learning in the classroom. She states:

Because Elizabeth is unselfish, she is willing to step back and to let the kids have the spotlight. For young teachers coming into the field it is very hard to do because they are insecure about where they are and what they're doing. In a very short period of time, she mastered that style of teaching. She lets them do much of the leading and she's always there to guide—that's an incredible gift. She gives them an awful lot to begin with, but they spend more time speaking and pro-ducing than she does in the classroom. Most of her work is done outside of the classroom. That's a really hard thing to do—to be able to be prepared enough, then to go forward and do it. The best exam-ple comes with a fifth-year Spanish class of Elizabeth's. As seniors, they don't want to be there and it's real tough. Some of the kids went on the Costa Rican exchange. They had work to do for Elizabeth while they were gone and one of the things they were working on was a play. Elizabeth knows this play backward and forward. In talking about it they said, "One of the great things is that this play could be so diffi-cult, and yet she makes it so easy for us by having us so well-prepared when we started—knowing the vocabulary, etc." As they started, they would, of course, say, "Is this the way this goes, is that the way it works?" And she would say to them, "Okay, think about what you've got. Think about what you just asked. Look at this part of it, see how that relates to what you just asked." Instead of answering their questions directly, she makes them dig it out. Then they asked, "Can we do some skits with these, can we write our own?" That doesn't happen if they're not feeling confident. She did incredible work with them in terms of pronunciation, content, and how to go about organizing the play scenes. After one term, they were so thrilled. They said, "Wow, we didn't realize we knew so much." I think this is the biggest compliment students can pay a teacher. They come saying, "This is so hard; I don't know anything." And they end up with, "Wow, I didn't realize I knew so much." It's a real tribute to her that they were able to feel that way at the end.

As a teacher, Elizabeth states her aim as "to teach my students how to learn to develop their intellectual skills, and also how to function socially and emotionally in a complex society. . . . I want them," she continues, "to feel good about themselves so they can develop their full potential." Her emphasis on intellectual and social development is illustrated in her discussion of a learning activity that brings out the best in her students.

I have one "core" activity which I modify to fit many different situations and which I find works for all levels. It combines the idea of cooperative learning with the goal of oral proficiency. I assign the students to write conversations in the target language. Sometimes they're structured, sometimes not; sometimes they have to write and perform them; sometimes they just say them in small groups spontaneously. For those who are timid, group gives them confidence and support. It gives all of them a sense of the usefulness of what they are learning. And for those that are more creative, they get a way to express themselves that is fun as well as constructive. Like any activity, there are days it works better than others, but I will continue to use and refine it.

Elizabeth states her belief about what is required to become a good foreign language teacher: "In addition to a thorough knowledge of the subject matter, a teacher needs to understand the learning processes and the emotional development specific to the age group he or she will teach. . . . It is most important," she stresses, "to understand the student as a person—an individual—until you accomplish that, you can't teach them."

In this line of thinking, Elizabeth believes that "the most important teaching skill is like a 'sixth sense'—to be able to sense the mood of the class as a whole or of an individual. As you sense it, you can adapt the class activity to fit the mood. Flexibility is very important, and a good sense of humor doesn't hurt either!"

Finally, her working classroom teaching philosophy involves challenging all students regardless of background to do their best work in her classes. In her daily teaching, she attempts to treat each student equally and respectfully, while encouraging students to live up their potential. She states:

> I'm a demanding teacher, with high expectations for all my students regardless of gender, race, or social background. I believe that the lower one's expectations, the less a student will achieve. Instead of giving the student confidence to try something more challenging, she or he senses that you feel she or he's "dumb" and will adapt to fit that image. While not varying my teaching for these differences, as part of my foreign language curriculum, I try to instill in my students a respect for cultural diversity.

EVALUATION

In assessing her strengths and weaknesses as a teacher, Elizabeth remarks: "I am organized, consistent, and fair; and I care very much about my students." She also indicates that she has "a lot of patience" and that she believes she "knows the kids pretty well" because she is close to them in age. "I know," she states, "where they're coming from and at this school there aren't a lot of young teachers. So they appreciate it."

She feels that she needs to improve by "continuing to develop the ability to adapt and be flexible. . . . Also, with more experience, I'll be better able to respond quickly to any situation that may arise in or out of class."

Her mentor and her supervisor speak of her strengths in glowing terms. Her informal mentor says that she is a perfectionist. "If she has done something on one day," the mentor asserts, "that she is not satisfied with we'll talk about it and decide how she could approach it again and deal with it in a different way. She'll go back until she feels she has done it to the best of her ability." According to her colleague, one of Elizabeth's major strengths is her ability to anticipate questions. "I think," the experienced teacher states, "that is remarkable for so young a teacher." She continues:

Elizabeth is also very clear in her explanations. If she's not here, students often come and say, "Is this all right? Mrs. Alberto said it was done this way. Am I doing it right?" I would say, "That's perfectly fine." And they would say, "Isn't that great! She taught us how to do it this way. Before it was so complicated. Now it's so easy."

Her mentor suggests that because of her fine organization and preparation, the students feel very comfortable in Elizabeth's classroom.

That's probably her real strength, building confidence in them. They are willing to take risks they wouldn't otherwise take. She had kids doing stuff this year in projects and independent work that was really exceptional. For instance, she had kids in their first year of Spanish do projects that third-year kids did not often attempt. Her students got up and did two- and four-minute skits. They wanted to videotape what they did, giving directions on how to do something or to get someplace. Usually, kids at the end of the first year are very reluctant to try to say anything in front of anyone else.

Her mentor feels that Elizabeth does not have any real weaknesses in the classroom. Rather, she states, "Elizabeth's biggest fault is that she works too hard. She gives too much of herself, and she's totally washed out. Whatever she does, she does 120 percent. It's very hard, then, to separate school life from family life."

Her department chair provides an informal but nonetheless insightful assessment of Elizabeth as a competent classroom teacher.

I have a personal test that I've used for years about checking in on how well I'm doing and how well other people are doing. It is the four-letter word test. If kids say to me that so-and-so is *good*, that so-and-so is *hard*, and so-and-so is *nice*, and that so-and-so is *fair*—that's very telling.

You don't need the word *funny*—that's nice if you have it; you don't need to come to every basketball game; you don't need to give out your phone number; you don't need to be called by your first name. Students are very perceptive, and I think that those four words, if they're all used with respect to the same person, are extremely telling. I have heard students talk about Elizabeth in that way. For that reason, I would say, then, that she's doing all right for herself.

Given these assessments, it is not surprising that Elizabeth is rated as an excellent beginning teacher by her principal, department chair, and informal mentor. She herself rates her first year of teaching as a great success. Her principal says that students, too, "recognize her as a superb teacher. Some kids complain occasionally because she is tough-minded. She won't let them get away with anything but she's still well-liked." The veteran teacher who serves as her mentor commented: "She is absolutely the best. She was the best-prepared beginning teacher I have ever seen." Her department chair agrees. She rates Elizabeth as the best beginning teacher she has worked with since becoming foreign language head four years earlier. She states:

> I've interviewed probably 15 candidates in different languages in the past few years. In the case of Elizabeth she was head and shoulders above anyone else that I've interviewed in her knowledge of what was happening in the profession, what a well-run classroom looks and feels like, and all the terminology and methods being used in foreign language teaching.
>
> One other thing that I should say about Elizabeth relates to an honor she recently received. In the fall of her first year at the high school, I got a letter asking me if I would like to nominate any young teacher for the outstanding foreign language teaching award that was given out by the Northeast Conference on the Teaching of Foreign Languages. I nominated Elizabeth. She didn't think she would have a chance. I said, "Well, you should try for it anyway." And she won! She won a fellowship to attend the annual conference. The fellowship paid for all of her expenses, and she was treated royally at the Conference. It was a nice professional experience for her.

Elizabeth, too, remarks about the importance of the award to her.

> I would like to mention the fellowship I won last year, which helped me through a difficult time when it seemed that I would not have a job for the 1990–91 school year. I was tired and feeling unappreciated. However, last year was the first time that the Northeast Conference on the Teaching of Foreign Languages offered a fellowship to pay for the hotel and registration fee, etc., to attend the spring conference in New York City. It was offered for beginning teachers—one for each of the northeastern states. I won the fellowship for Massachusetts. The Conference in April helped me to re-energize and reaffirm my goals in teaching. It's not just the teachers with years of experience that feel disenamored of the profession at times. There should be more opportunities such as this to encourage young teachers to continue in the profession.

Finally, Elizabeth discussed her first year on the job. Her comments reflect her pragmatic and realistic perspective.

I think the first year of teaching in and of itself has to be one of survival—of simply getting through the material. The second year, when you've established your "reputation" and when the many rules and clerical matters become automatic, then you can afford to be more creative and really improve your teaching style.

The first year is also difficult because it's a bit of a disappointment when you learn the "reality" of being a teacher. So much of your time is spent on unimportant (in terms of creating an exciting learning experience for kids) things like administrative, clerical duties, hall duty, cafeteria duty, etc. I think my situation is better than that of other teachers because my school is well-known for its dedication to a quality education. Yet, even here the teacher is expected to do all these other things—of course, there's no one else to do it.

However, having a good class makes up for so much of the frustrations that I have mentioned. A good day means classes where I feel connected with the students and, therefore, they have learned something. A good day means students come to see me during extra help time, either for help or just to discuss some triumph or problem with me. That's what makes it all worthwhile.

POSTSCRIPT

Like Wendy and CW, Elizabeth was riffed or laid off during her first and second year of teaching. However, in both academic years she was rehired by the school system. She continues her summer visits to her husband's family in Spain.

CHAPTER 5

Teacher as Storyteller: Maria Fernandez

Maria Fernandez, an Hispanic, taught science her first year in a large New York City school. She grew up and has lived most of her life in the city. As a single parent in her forties, she has raised two children, a son of 22 and a daughter of 19. Her interest in teaching came quite late in her life and almost by happenstance. Several years ago, when completing her bachelor's degree at Columbia University, the dean of general studies suggested she pursue teaching as a career. She explained his rationale and her response.

> Because I didn't have any career plans and geology, my major, was not really good those days for jobs, he said, "Well, why don't you try going for the education program at Barnard, and you can teach science in high school or in junior high school." And I said, "Well, okay." The first day of student teaching, I knew that I was in love. I came back to my home and all I could say was, "I'm in love with kids." I couldn't express it any other way. It was suddenly finding something about myself that I never even knew I had inside of me.

Her children were supportive of her decision to teach. Maria says they're "kind of proud. My daughter tells everybody I'm a geologist who teaches kids." Maria relates that she raised her kids in a democratic fashion.

> I never put rules in front of my kids, except rules that had a basis, that were thoroughly explained and had a rationale behind them. When I said to my son when he was young, "Don't cross the street," I never said, "because I said so" or "because I'm your mother." But I said, "Cars go by here. When you get hit by a car, a car will kill you." I know it's a simple explanation but there's always a rationale. My home is a democratic home. My children have a voice in my home as well as I have a voice. We never make decisions without everybody's input.
>
> I learned these things from experience. My mother was always

saying to me, "I said so," or even before I had a chance to explain certain things, I was getting beat and feeling so offended by that behavior that I knew that just wasn't the way I wanted to be with my own children. When I see how my children have grown up, then I know that I can use the same tactics with my students and it works.

In high school, Maria had several teachers who served as role models for her in both positive and negative senses. She relates:

When I think about it and when I evaluate the type of teacher that I am trying to be, I always look at those qualities in these teachers, and the things that I saw in them were how supportive, how loving, how caring they were to me as a person. And then how challenging the experiences I had with them in the classroom. These were teachers who wanted to make a difference in the kids by being nice to them. In turn, that's the kind of teacher I am trying to be.

One of them was Mrs. Mullins who was a math teacher. I was the worst in math in school. But when I was in her class, she made me feel that I could do it. I went on to another class after that believing that I could do it, and I met up with Mr. Barrett, who made me feel totally intimidated. I left math, there and then. Basically, he just took care of the white kids and ignored me. Therefore, I had two teachers in the same subject—one that turned me on to math and another who turned me off. If I had taken math the next semester with Mrs. Mullins, I would probably be a math teacher today.

She just took an interest. She explained things really well and worked with me after school. She was the kind of teacher who at Christmas time, invited me to come to her home. She also got me a job in the school. I was volunteering as a helper in the art department and she found a way for me to get paid for that work. She took me to see the Salvador Dali exhibit when it was in New York. These were really important things in my life. I was into art but at the same time because of the way she was I got into the math.

The urban high school where Maria teaches has a population of over 3,000 students and a faculty of over 300 teachers. In the first semester, Maria taught five classes to ninth graders in physical science and earth science, including a bilingual section in the latter subject. Almost all of the students are Hispanics or African-Americans. The faculty is composed of primarily white, older teachers, many of whom are nearing retirement. Maria describes the school as one with a strict discipline regimen.

Because of budget cuts caused by low student attendance, Maria was almost laid off in second semester. She explains:

Every year—it's so weird what happens in those schools—at the end of the semester if you are not a full-time teacher—but a temporary per diem appointment as I was, they give you a letter saying "sorry but, we have to dispense with you." I was the newest teacher in the department. Surprisingly enough, the principal cut people who had been there before me. But at the very end, the last day before the second semester was going to start, he called the department chair and said: "What has come down the tubes—and I am really sorry this is happening—is that we will probably have to get rid of Maria." And everybody—the older teachers—just went, "Oh, no!" I knew the principal had been trying not to let me go. He said, "We're going to try anything that we can to keep you here. Just come in on Monday and at least you can work next week. We'll try to do whatever we can. We'll see what we can finagle." I think it was only last week [in late February] that he finally said, "Okay, you are staying."

In order to maintain her on the staff, Maria was given a "comp time" position. Her teaching schedule was reduced to three ninth-grade physical science courses, and she became coordinator of the Attendance Improvement Dropout Prevention Program in which she counseled for two periods a day. Beside her counseling, this program for at-risk students involved her in various field trips to Yankee Stadium and to plays. Once a month she went into their classes to give the students small gifts for staying in school.

During the academic year she was assigned a buddy teacher, a veteran science teacher, who was given released time to help mentor Maria in the classroom. While he was helpful to Maria, she increasingly came to confide in her department chair, a veteran science teacher near retirement. Unfortunately, the science head died before he could be interviewed about Maria's first year of teaching. The principal, who was also supportive of her as a teacher, retired the following year.

FIRST DAY OF TEACHING

Maria discusses her first day of teaching as one of some anxiety and some nurturing.

I had instructions from my department on what to do on the first day of class. They specifically told me to hand out the program cards— they were very mechanical things that I had to do, so I wasn't really confronted with teaching the first day. What I did feel was that, "How do these kids see me? What am I representing here?"

Because these ninth-grade kids were brand-new in the high

school, they were just as scared as I was. So instead of thinking how scared I was, I tried to alleviate the feelings that they were having by making them feel comfortable and, straight off the bat, let them know that I was a nice person. I care about kids. "And as long as you show me the same kind of respect, the same care, there will be no problem in the classroom, we can all work together." So after the mechanical stuff, I immediately told them the kind of person that I would try to be with them. I told them, "I am a very nice teacher but if you overstep your boundaries, I am going to sit on your face." And they all laughed because they cannot imagine how anybody would sit on their face.

They know that it was a joke in some ways but they also came to know that I mean what I say. I don't really delineate boundaries of behavior, per se, but they know when they see my face, they know. I don't go berating them too much. I look at them in a certain way and they know when I am looking that way. For some reason they caught onto that really quickly that they would rather be nice than not nice.

CLASSROOM TEACHING PERSONA

As a teacher, Maria is described by her buddy teacher as an "enthusiastic, knowledgeable, and even youthful" teacher who has "excellent rapport" with students. She herself hopes that she is looked upon by students as

a caring teacher—somebody that is able to motivate and challenge them and at the same time understand them and be able to give them guidance not just in my subject area but in life in general. Because so many of their mothers are working, I feel that kids often lack a certain direction—a little support. I love to excite them about the subject matter but also to help them whenever they need some nurturing.

In talking about her special teaching mission, Maria states:

Where I teach is one of the toughest areas. I asked to be given the worst classes—the lower levels. I did have a couple of good classes of regular students. Tracks in New York City are regular or modified. I requested to be given modified classes because I thought I would have a better chance of influencing those kids. I didn't think the regular kids needed the type of teacher I am as much as the modified kids did. The effectiveness of my teaching was better used by them. They needed all the help they could get. I thought I would be more useful to them, than to the regular kids. Anybody can teach them.

In her classes she treated all students respectfully and, regardless of race or IQ, "tried to involve all kids equally and to reach each kid individually."

TEACHING APPROACH

In detailing her teaching metaphor, Maria discusses her classroom role as facilitator and as storyteller. These dual roles are essential, she believes, in helping meet her students' learning needs and in providing relevance and personal meaning in their academic lives.

I'm a team player. I like to get my kids thinking that we are all in it together. That I am there to just facilitate how they look at the subject matter and who they become. I try to help them think through things.

I'm not there as the boss and you're the student. The first thing I do when I walk into class is say, "Your opinion here is as sacred as mine. You have a right to say what you feel and nobody has the right to shoot somebody down for what they say. Yes, there will be limits—there will be situations in which you have to respect one another. You will not curse or be disrespectful." I try to teach them the meaning of respect. It is not that "I'm the boss and you're the student" but that "I have sensibilities as well as you that may be offended by your behavior." Therefore, you will be careful how you handle yourself and carry yourself in the classroom. If you do manage to offend somebody, then you apologize. Those are the rules in the classroom. In spite of my openness, I am still the person who has to manage.

It is, of course, difficult to implement this style of teaching in an urban high school since you have a set curriculum to cover and the textbooks don't cover the material. Thus I give demonstrations and the students think about what is happening. They observe, and then I describe exactly what they are seeing. For instance, put some carbonate in a jar and them dump some acid on it and have the kids observe the chemical reaction. "Tell me what you think is happening." At another time, I wrote on the board the different properties of matter. I defined the properties for them. Then I went through with them what each property meant. Next I gave them different pieces of matter—some rocks, some metal, and other elements. I had them evaluate the materials using the guidelines that I gave on the board, identifying it and using all of the properties listed. So I'm not only teaching them how to think but to observe—teaching them the process.

To make the material more academically viable for them, I tell them my own stories or personal experiences that relate directly to

science. You know, "Here is one of Mrs. F's stories!" Ooohhhh! It got
to be one of those jokes in the classroom. I say, "This is another one."
I told them a story about flammable things in chemistry. How can I
tell them about "flammable"? They know what flammable is! How
can I make it interesting? So I tell them about my friend wanting to
burn a bunch of leaves in the country and the leaves not wanting to
burn so quickly. Another friend told her to put gasoline on it. So she
makes a little trail of gasoline to the leaf pile and lit up the little end
of the trail. All of a sudden, no sooner had she lit the trail, than this
whole thing went up in smoke, threw her back on her butt, and burned
her eyelashes and her hair. "Hey! that is a true story!"

It is a dramatic thing for them to realize that you cannot just
light up gasoline. I also bring the movies up. "Remember when you
saw this movie when the guy went with the car into the gas station
and then it exploded?" Then I relate it to other things. "Why do you
think that they ask you not to smoke a cigarette in the gas station?"
These are not the kids that would be really interested in technical
stuff. So I try to relate it to their everyday experience so that they
may actually feel what is going on.

You may want to teach science and math but unless you are able
to relate it to life—how it applies to a child's everyday life—that child
is not going to get it unless he or she sees that there is a point in
learning what you're teaching. If not, that child is not going to get it.
For myself, I take every opportunity, in general, to try to help kids
with their lives. For instance, in science, I had to teach about the
reproductive system. The point came when the kids were laughing
and giggling when I was talking about the male and female reproductive systems. At that point I took the opportunity to talk about safe
sex. I didn't just say, "Okay, here's that, here's this," and that's the
end of it. All of a sudden, there came questions from the kids. You
have to be ready to explain those questions. And when you explain
them, give also another message.

In discussing what she really is trying to do in the classroom, Maria
elaborates on her working philosophy of teaching.

I'm trying to excite students about the subject matter—plain and simple. If a child in any way feels that perhaps he or she wants to do
science, I want him or her to feel that he or she can do it. Science, in
particular, is something too many people feel intimidated by. I look
back at myself and the example I gave about the two math teachers.
What I want to accomplish is what Mrs. Mullins did for me. I want to
do that in terms of science and math because I have to teach math at
the same time I teach science. Math is the language of science. If

there is an inkling in your mind as a student that you want to do science, I don't want you to be turned off by it.

For example, there was one girl who came to see me the very first day of classes in the first semester. She said, "Mrs. Fernandez, I want you to know that I'm not good in science. I've never done good at science and I'm not planning to do good at science." I responded, "Why don't you give yourself a chance?" She ended up acing the course. But it took a lot of working with her, a lot of support and saying, "You can do it, you can do it, you can do it. You'll see!" To me, science is really important, probably the most important thing in life.

Maria believes that an educator needs a great deal of knowledge and refined communication and listening skills to be the kind of teacher she is in the classroom. She relates:

I'm a very well-rounded person. I have no compunction in saying that. I'm not bragging. I have a very deep education. I can do anything: science, math, art, psychology. You name it and I have a background in it. You have to be broad if you want to be a really effective teacher.

You also have to be a clown. You have to be able to laugh—laugh at any situation and be flexible.

Most of all, you must be empathetic. You have to be tuned to moods. You have to have lots of psychology or, better, an understanding of human nature. You may have a kid that comes in one day and his or her head is down. Instead of saying, "Put your head up," you have to come very quietly in an empathetic manner. I would come and put my hand on the person's shoulder and whisper, "Hey, are you okay? Is there anything I can do for you? Are you feeling bad? Do you want to talk to me afterwards?" At that moment or later, they have a chance to explain to me why they are doing that. Rather than like some teachers saying, "Hey! Why are you going to sleep in my class?" I try initially to give them the benefit of the doubt so they don't feel threatened and don't have to be belligerent about it. If I'm belligerent first, they will be belligerent back. Instead, I show that I'm willing to listen to whatever story they have. If they say, "I'm not feeling well today," I would say, "Rest a bit. When you feel ready to listen, I would like you to participate." I do it in a humane manner. If the kid is being plain mean, then I would take the kid aside, altogether.

Some of my kids end up being chatty at times. Because of the teacher that I am that does happen. I work under controlled chaos at all times—which is good for me. I like the kids being able to feed in. No matter what it is that they are feeding into the class, I like the fact that they are not just sitting around, staring into space. They communicate with each other about the classwork. They communicate with me, whether it is about something that happened outside of the classroom or within the classroom. But they know when I say, "Okay, let's continue the lesson," that they do pipe down. Sometimes it gets kind of hairy but, basically, it is not a big problem. I try to use the energy level that they have rather than try to squash it. I don't waste it. Obviously that energy has to be good for something.

In discussing her toughest problems as a first-year teacher, Maria also reveals an interrelated problem that faces new, highly idealistic teachers. How do you change the conduct of other faculty whose views and teaching style are offensive to your values and to the norms of good practice? How do you change the views and self-perceptions of students who have been influenced and turned off by such teachers? She relates:

I wish I could do something about an old-time teacher who shares a room with me. One day I hadn't left the room yet. All his kids were coming in and he came in. As soon as he entered the room, he lit into the kids and started calling them "morons." For what, I don't know. He just lit into these kids. "You morons, you stupid such and such." I just turned around, looked at the kids, and I said to them, "It's all right," and just walked out. I felt like saying, "I apologize to you guys for this asshole."

How do you deal with people who are so offensive to the kids, and then complain that the kids don't come to school? If I reported him, it wouldn't do any good. He's got two years before he retires. He has always had problems with the school but he is still there. So what do you do?

My toughest problem is controlling kids. No, let me restate it. Convincing the kids that I wasn't like the rest of the teachers that had taught them before.

Trying to break the habit that they had of not having a voice in the classroom. Convincing them that they had a voice in my classroom. That whatever they had to say was valid. That was probably the hardest thing for them to learn. That I wasn't going to put them down, that I wasn't going to be a sexist with them. That I wasn't going to be calling them morons and jerks.

EVALUATION

In describing her strengths as a teacher, Maria confesses that she, too, has a great deal of energy. "I have a lot of energy and I don't hesitate to jump around the room," she admits. "I will do just anything that I can to get them excited about what they are learning." She continues, "I think science is an exciting field and I think I can communicate it to them; it's not the doldrums to me, it is something I love. My principal wrote me a letter saying, 'You are a great motivator of children.' I hope he is right because that is what I intend to be—a motivator."

Her weaknesses as a teacher relate to her inexperience and her continual need for self-improvement. She says:

> I need to learn the material more. I have the basics for geology but I am faced with teaching chemistry and physics, which are not my strong points. I also want to learn to do really great demonstrations. At this point, my demonstrations are mostly improvised. I bring materials into class but they are not as good as I know they can be.

Finally, Maria wants to learn even more about teaching in general. "I just want," she states, "to continue becoming a good teacher. I always ask questions of other teachers and administrators. I want to know! I want to know—sometimes I feel, 'Well, God, what should I be learning now?'"

Maria is rated by her mentors as a first-year teacher with "excellent potential." Her buddy teacher relates that because of her "subject-matter expertise," her "hard work," and her ability to "relate very well" to kids, if she continues teaching she will do quite well. She, too, feels proud of her accomplishments as a beginning teacher. As she states, "I am exhilarated! I am very happy being a teacher." Many of her students also are pleased at having Maria as a teacher. Maria relates, "By second semester the kids already know about you. One kid stood up in class and said, 'Yo, she's chill!' That was all I needed. What better recommendation could I get?" Another testimony to her as a fine person and caring professional relates to her "open door" policy during her free periods in school.

> Whenever I could, I would sit in the classroom and have open doors for students to come in whenever they wanted. Eighth period was my free period and I would have 25 kids in the classroom. The kids would talk about whatever they wanted to talk about. There were times on holidays when teachers would let them go from their classes or kids would play hookey. They would come to my classes and I would have a full classroom of students—talking.

Finally, Maria provides these insights and advice to beginning teachers, particularly those contemplating teaching in urban schools.

> Be open to the kids. Be there for them. Make rules. Kids need the rules, you know that. But be prepared to believe them sometimes when they tell you a story and be open to them because they need

people. I am talking more from the perspective of being in New York City. A lot of kids in New York schools have horrible family lives and when they come to school, it is probably the safest place they can find. They need somebody to say, "You're okay." Be accepting of them. Be supportive when they do something nice.

I teach ninth grade, which is the grade everybody says, "Oh, no!" to, but I love it. I love the excitement that they bring to the classroom. I think little kids need to have somebody who is calm, who is sweet and nice. Because they are full of excitement and energy, you've got to be receptive to that and give it right back to them. Otherwise you bore the hell out of them—you know.

POSTSCRIPT

At the conclusion of her first year, Maria resigned from her urban school to pursue a master's degree in science education at Pennsylvania State University. She is now enrolled in a doctoral program in earth science at the university. In summer 1990, she was project coordinator of the "Best Program," a summer school program at the university for gifted minority students in science and mathematics. The program was sponsored by Eastman Kodak to recruit more minority students into these fields.

PART II

The Dynamics of Teaching:
The Realities

Reflecting on the four portraits of beginning teachers reveals distinct differences in temperament and some differences in emphasis in their teaching. They, of course, also present different teaching perspectives based in part on different values, training, and backgrounds. Yet, these four beginners also share in common many attributes: a deep personal commitment to students, the willingness to devote considerable time and resources to achieving their teaching missions, and a vitality and energy that have an uplifting effect on students as well as on other faculty and administrators. All four teachers are, of course, articulate and seem to have a certain degree of cognitive sophistication as problem solvers that is at times surprising for rookie teachers. Finally, they are quick learners and self-starters who often take the lead both in and outside the classroom. It is this combination of high personal energy, commitment, brainpower, and initiative that makes these four teachers and many others in the study special, but not unique, beginning teachers.

Moreover, in many ways these beginning teachers have already internalized and acted on a fundamental tenet of good teaching. As James Comer (cited in Gursky, 1990) states, "Learning is not only a mechanical process. Relationships are also important to learning, and that's what we haven't given enough attention to" (p. 47). In a similar vein, Robert Coles (1990) quotes William Carlos Williams, the medical doctor and novelist, about what makes a good teacher or person. "What else is there, finally, but one person making a difference to another?" (p. 59). These four teachers have made a difference to many of their students and colleagues who have worked with them in their initial year of teaching. They also share similar views of what constitutes good teaching, as do the other beginning teachers in this study. All of the 37 beginners view teaching and learning as dynamic processes that call forth, clarify, and challenge their emerging professional identities. In striving to meet high standards of performance in their daily teaching, these beginners also confront and must deal with practical realities and constraints of the classroom and school environments. Adapting to the new realities while struggling to maintain their idealism and enthusiasm is the focus of part II of the book.

In Chapter 6, the beginners' views of good teaching and their assessment of their own teaching effectiveness, particularly with at-risk students, are presented. Chapter 7 focuses on the problems and dilemmas of the beginning teacher—their nature, their seriousness, and their urgency, particularly with regard to questions of classroom control and authority. Chapter 8 considers the critical issues of curriculum and evaluation decision making. Chapter 9 centers on the professional concerns and the "cycle of teaching" for the beginner as well as the more experienced teacher. Chapter 10 examines the mentoring of novice teachers and its personal and professional importance in helping newcomers learn the ropes of classroom teaching. Chapter 11 concludes with a summary of findings and recommendations on how to improve the inservice education and the first-year experience of beginning teachers.

CHAPTER 6

Views of Good Teaching

In this chapter, the general discussion will focus on what beginners view as good teaching. The first section will deal with the active learning model of teaching that almost all the beginners advocate and practice. The second section will review the criteria they employ for judging good teaching and their own effectiveness in the classroom with all students, but especially with unmotivated and difficult-to-handle adolescents.

ACTIVE LEARNING: A MODEL OF TEACHING

As the four portraits in Part I illustrate so clearly, it is difficult to categorize novice teachers into any one philosophical view of teaching. Their classroom perspectives and the working knowledge that they employ in the classroom not only are composite of diverse elements derived from observation, study, and past practice as student teachers, but are also dynamic and changing in response to their specific school context and daily classroom teaching. Thus, it is somewhat problematic to generalize about new teachers who are forming and re-forming a view of their role in the classroom. However, some statements can be made that seem to capture the broad outlines of an emerging model of teaching that almost all the nearly 40 beginners who participated in the study seem to share. This model emphasizes active learning along with student autonomy and social responsibility. Two beginning teachers got at the heart of this view of classroom teaching as they responded to the question, "What am I really trying to do with students?"

Second-year Suburban English Teacher
I guess really making them independent learners and not just passive receivers. Getting them to think instead of just putting down information. It sounds so simple. But the way a lot of schools are set up, it's just they take in information, they spit it back and the faster they spit it back—that's the way it's reflected on their report card. Thinking

isn't really there; nor are people working cooperatively to solve problems.

I'm trying to get students to be willing to take a risk in class and know it's okay to take a risk and fail once in a while. I am also working to get students to trust each other. Basically, they don't treat each other the way they should, and a lot of the time it's because they're not real secure themselves. I try and work that environment out—let kids get a better sense of themselves.

First-year Rural Science Teacher

In science, it is to teach kids the skills of science. Processing science—not necessarily to memorize facts but to see the big picture and relate it to the world. For kids, four years seems so long for them as ninth graders, so long to get out into the world. But it's not, and boom they're there. If we can show them the process of science—which maybe helps them process other skills as well—that will help them as adults to become better citizens. There are so many things out there you don't need to know until you have a problem. If you know how to access, you can get your hands on it.

The old way of science is, "Here's your list of vocabulary. Read it, memorize it, and spit it back out on the test." The new way is, "This is all the knowledge we know and this is how I'm going to show you how to access it—the computer, the library, periodicals. Things like that." And, finally, in the ninth grade, to get them from the concrete operational to the next step. "Let's see what we can see, not only right here in our hands but in our minds."

Both of these young teachers have clear goals for their classroom teaching. Like other novices in the study, they share a strong belief in helping their students learn to think critically on their own or with their peers when confronting new problems and circumstances. In Jackson's (1987) terms, their ultimate goal of "self-governance" for their students involves adolescents "learning to learn" and "choosing to learn" (p. 45). As Jackson indicates and these teachers' comments echo, helping students learn to learn implies equipping adolescent learners with the "tools and resources" that will help them attain their learning goals. For the beginners, it involves helping their students master higher-order reasoning in action—assessing, analyzing, and evaluating information—as well as such attitudes as "respect for others" in the classroom community and "self-confidence" in one's own ability to take risks (p. 49). Choosing to learn, of course, refers to the "process of selecting goals of learning, choosing what is to be learned, whether with the help of teachers or on one's own" (p. 49). While both the senior high English teacher and the junior high science teacher believe that such independent decision making is the ultimate goal, the ninth-grade science teacher certainly understands the developmental nature of the task. Her view is in line with that expressed by another junior high school teacher: "So it's helping give them that step that they can take further when they're more mature."

One other aspect of this model of teaching relates to what Jackson calls "painless pedagogy." A young history teacher defines it this way: "My big goal is to try to teach eighth graders some responsibility and some ownership for their learning. And to try to get them interested and see that school can be interesting and it can be fun." An English teacher spells out in more detail this emphasis on "fun" learning. "We get to do lots of fun things like debates, which they love to do, or other active things like writing a fifth chapter to *The Red Pony* because a lot of them didn't like the way it ended. We spent a couple of days on that and that was just a fun thing where they could do something creative."

Of course, not all beginning teachers in the sample professed the "inquiry problem-solving" approach of these new teachers. As one mathematics teacher stated:

> I'm concerned that they'll go all the way through their school careers and not have the fundamentals—decimals, fractions, a sense of numbers. This is where they get it. I really have a crusade for that. That they understand such essential concepts so that they're prepared to go whichever way they want—high school, college prep, whatever. They all need that.

This mathematics teacher's more traditional emphasis on the "basics" is also informed by his understanding about the nature of early adolescents. "It is easy to get caught up in content," he continues, "but I have to resist that—it's not where they're at. It's important that school is a good experience for them. We can turn them off very easily in seventh and eighth grade." While his substantive emphasis is different from that of the teacher who focuses more on the processes of learning, his concern for students' psychological and social development is similar. As this mathematics teacher puts it, "Understand the customers. The customers are the kids at the level they're at. It's useful math we're after." Dewey could not have agreed more.

Thus in this study of beginning teachers there are at least two models of caring novice teachers: the more traditional teacher who stresses basic skill training and the acquisition of core knowledge, and the more "progressive" teacher who emphasizes the acquisition of information—processing skills and meaningful knowledge of both a substantive and personal nature. Both types of teachers share a concern to make the subject matter relevant and to make learning as enjoyable as possible.

The majority of the beginning teachers in the sample, however, appear to be eclectic in their teaching style—at times drawing upon both views of teaching. In *A Place Called School*, Goodlad (1984) comes to the same conclusion about the larger sample of elementary, junior high, and high school teachers in his study. "At all three levels of schooling these teachers—like other teachers, according to other studies—endorsed traditional and progressive beliefs simultaneously" (p. 174). Specifically, when asked to characterize their teaching style, the group of 38 teachers responded in this fashion: Six identified their style as "more process-oriented (skill development, asking questions, etc.)"; four defined their style as "mostly content-oriented (facts, concepts, interpretations, etc.)"; and 28 characterized their style as "process and content equally stressed." Wendy Light, Elizabeth Alberto, Maria Fernandez, and James Crawford-Williams were in this last category.

Given the highly contextualized nature of classroom teaching, it is not surprising that the majority of beginning teachers are pragmatic—informed by the standard of "what works." Beginners acquire this practical and flexible approach in large part from what Lortie (1975) has termed the "apprenticeship of observation," the thousands of hours they have put in watching teachers from grade school through college or graduate school, and also from the cooperating teachers who supervised their student teaching. In many ways, the cooperating teacher is the strongest influence on the student teacher's professional training, and this influence, as in Wendy Light's and other cases, is likely to carry over to the first-year teaching situation. For example, one beginning teacher described her cooperating teacher as

> a very good teacher but she's not obsessive. She does her lesson plans; she flies with them; she handwrites out a lot of stuff. She's not hooked on having to do everything perfectly, but she does a wonderful job. She figures it out as she goes along; if something doesn't work, she says, "Well, that didn't work, we'll try something different next time." She's been teaching for 20 years and she'll still change stuff.

It appears from classroom observation and interviews with this novice teacher that she, too, has adopted these attitudes in her role as a secondary social studies teacher.

TEACHING EFFECTIVENESS

In determining how teachers go about assessing their classroom effectiveness, a number of questions were asked of the beginners about their strong and weak points as teachers, their criteria for judging a good lesson and for determining how well students are doing, and their personal sense of efficacy in motivating "adolescents at risk" in their school. Whenever possible, their answers are compared with the responses of the experienced teachers who participated in the study.

While these qualitative data are rich in texture and meaning, there are also limitations to self-reporting. As Cronbach (1990) points out, "The self-report is . . . a deliberate self-presentation" and often represents an image a person wishes to project (p. 513). "Candid reporting may be hoped for," he contends, in certain circumstances, including research studies. "Investigators can hope for an honest effort to introspect; subjects want to explain themselves. But even then it is natural to give responses that will be judged favorably insofar as respondents can guess the investigator's standards for judgement" (p. 514). How accurate, then, are the beginning teachers' assessments of their own teaching performance? This is, of course, an open question that can never be fully answered. Complicating the research issue is that there is evidence suggesting that even experienced teachers have difficulty portraying accurately what they do in the classroom. However, Cronbach points out that even when individuals in self-reports present too perfect an image, it tells us something about the individual's personality and perhaps his or her typical pattern of behavior.

Given these restraints and precautions, the self-reports of the beginners in the study seem candid and consistent with the classroom perspectives that they revealed through their interviews, their written questionnaire responses, and my observations of many of them in the classroom. As data in the four case studies indicate, the mentors of these four teachers also believe that the beginners have a good sense of their own relative strengths and weaknesses as teachers. Of course, there remains an element of subjectivity that must be weighed in considering the beginners' self-appraisals of their classroom teaching effectiveness.

Self-Assessment

The beginning teachers interviewed were asked to identify their strong and weak points as teachers. This general self-assessment is useful in determining not only how the beginners evaluate their own teaching, but how their professional preparation might be improved. Here are lists of perceived strengths and weaknesses generated by three first-year teachers.

While these comments are typical of other teachers in the survey, care was taken to include the perspectives of suburban, rural, and urban teachers from two subject areas.

First-Year Rural English Teacher

Strong points. My sense of humor—A lot of teachers would get bugged by some of the things kids say, and I just let it roll off.

Being young—I think the kids can relate to me and can talk to me a lot better.

I'm fair—I don't have any favorites, everyone gets a fair shake, pretty much; you always get a second chance.

Needed areas of improvement. I could improve in discipline and organization of time. I don't know if any teacher is happy with his or her organization of time. I feel I've developed ways to do things more effectively, but there are still ways that I need to improve. When I first started, I'd waste five minutes of the class handing out papers. Now I know that they can be reading something while you're handing out papers. Budgeting, planning my classroom time more efficiently is perhaps a better way to describe the problem.

First-Year Urban Social Studies Teacher

Strong points. I can sit back and allow my kids to communicate their ideas and not always want to interfere and tell them what I think. I also feel that I have developed good rapport with them—that I'm not trying to be smarter than them. Rather, I'm a resource person for my students. They can come to me and bounce ideas off me, and I can help them play with their ideas as opposed to being the dominant expert who lectures them and tells them what to do.

Needed areas of improvement. I think I can always improve on helping them develop their own ideas. I still feel I give them too much and don't allow them to take on enough responsibility. I'm working on that, and I'm always thinking: "How do I want to do it so they don't need me?"

First-Year Suburban Social Studies Teacher

Strong points. I get along with and relate well with the students— part of it is my age; I hope that gift doesn't change with age; part of it is because I appreciate that there are days when things are tough. I try to get involved as much as I can outside the classroom, and I think that helps in the classroom.

I'm really conscientious. I could not look in the mirror if I walked into a classroom unprepared; it's something that I think is a disgrace to the profession. So I try to prepare the best I can for every class and not waste the students' time.

I think I have a creative sense in the classroom. I'm more than willing to try group activities or simulations, and I love doing the stuff.

Needed areas of improvement. Grading skill—sometimes I have problems with reading essays. What's the difference between 82 and 84? If two students came to me and said why did I get an 86 and why did I get an 80, I'm not sure that if I reread the essays I could give them a good reason. I hope I'm fair, but I sometimes feel a little inexperienced putting a grade on, especially subjective things like essays. I usually have some criteria, but it's just so subjective, and I think it influences it when I see the name on the paper. For example, if someone hasn't been doing well and all of a sudden he or she writes something well, I might be willing to give the person an 85; or if someone who usually gets a high 80 does something poor—poorer than he or she usually does—I might give the student an 80. However, the 80 grade of the better student is probably better than the 85 grade of the usually poorer student. That I really need to work on. I hope it comes with experience.

These self-assessments seem honest and balanced presentations of the teachers' public selves. They reveal the plurality of "virtues and vices" of many beginners. The strengths of these beginning teachers lie in their intellectual skills and in their character. In his seminal works on the eight stages of the life cycle, Erikson (1963) defines "basic virtue" in its traditional sense: "inherent strength" or "active quality . . . which begins to animate man pervasively during successive stages of his life" (p. 3). "Virtue and spirit," he points out, "once had interchangeable meanings" (Erikson, 1964, p. 113). He orders these basic human qualities in this way.

I will, therefore, speak of Hope, Will, Purpose, and Competence as the rudiments of virtue developed in childhood; of Fidelity as the adolescent virtue; and of Love, Care, and Wisdom as the central virtues of adulthood. Each virtue and its place in the schedule of all virtues is vitally interrelated to other segments of human development. (p. 114)

This combination of childhood and adolescent virtues and the adult virtues of platonic love and care are at the core of the beginning teacher's constitution. These "vital virtues" plus the beginning teachers' enthusiasm for teaching, their sense of fairness, and their empathy, sensitivity, and commitment to their students are at the "rock bottom" of their emerging professional identity. They are on schedule in their personal and professional development. Equally important, as spirited novices, they are consciously and earnestly seeking the "practical wisdom" required to be a good teacher and self-actualized adult.

An individual's weaknesses as well as his or her strengths help define the teacher as a professional. These newcomers' perceived limitations are not fundamental weaknesses. Rather, in most cases their problems stem from a lack of reflection and experience. The beginners often cite logistical concerns—better procedures for planning or organizing classroom time or activities—as refinements that they need to incorporate into their daily teaching. Even the question of grading objectively and fairly can be managed (but perhaps not solved) with more practice and with universalistic as opposed to particularistic criteria of assessment. It is at this level—the tough issue of assessment—that both preservice and inservice training could be improved.

It is not enough for teacher educators or school administrators only to commiserate with the beginner about the difficulty of grading "unequals equitably." Required courses on assessment and evaluation or on teaching the unmotivated are not really necessary. But more sustained dialogue and more reflection on the part of the beginning teacher on these vital matters are prerequisites. Moreover, most beginning teachers want help. As one first-year teacher said about his teacher preparation program:

> Evaluating students came up a lot in our seminar discussions: "How do you learn to grade?" The answer was, "Grade and hopefully you'll get better at it." Another answer was to have other teachers read a few of them and compare things. That sounds good but, in reality, if someone handed me 10 essays, I'd say I just don't have time to do it, and that unfortunately happens.

In this regard, we can all do better in conveying the "wisdom of practice" to our protégés or inexperienced colleagues. For instance, an early September beginning-teacher workshop led by experienced and second- and third-year teachers can be very valuable to new teachers. At such a workshop, the critical questions of student assessment can be raised, and the beginners will have an opportunity to reflect on how their more senior colleagues have handled such tough issues in the past. The workshop will also provide the newcomers with important information on the norms and practices of grading in their secondary school.

Judging Classroom Effectiveness

What criteria do beginning teachers employ to judge their effectiveness in the classroom? Two survey questions help get at the implicit and explicit standards novices and veteran teachers adopt to judge how well their teaching is going. The first question, "What are your criteria of a good class?"

relates to the factors or indicators teachers utilize to judge the success or impact of a daily lesson. The second question, "How do you gauge the effectiveness of your teaching?" is a more comprehensive question, which Lortie used in his study of Dade County (Florida) teachers described in *Schoolteacher* (1975). His data on first- and second-year teachers and experienced teachers can be compared with the beginners' and veteran teachers' responses in this study.

The criteria for evaluating the effectiveness of a daily class, of course, varied according to the teacher's classroom teaching perspective, the teaching discipline, and the school context. But these differences are often matters more of degree than of kind. There appears to be an emerging consensus on the part of beginners and veterans on a general standard. Here are the criteria listed by two novices and two experienced teachers who teach in different school environments and at different grade levels.

First-Year English Teacher in Rural High School
   Most kids are doing the "stuff" well.
   They are hopefully getting something out of it.
   They get it.
   They are having a good time.

Veteran English Teacher in Rural High School
   Shared sense of fun.
   Mutual respect.
   Energy and enthusiasm.
   Student works hard because he/she knows that I believe in him/her.

Second-Year Math Teacher in Urban Experimental School
   When the kids have clear directions.
   They move through the lesson.
   The teacher has enough time to coach them when needed and to keep
      records of what went on with each kid: "so-and-so" understood
      this concept, "so-and-so" needs to work on this one.

Veteran Science Teacher in Independent Middle School
   One that stimulates the students by asking them questions and allowing
      them to ask me questions.
   Sense of objectives is clearly stated to all.
   Enthusiasm and preparation of student and teacher are evident.

One common element of a successful class is the criterion of work. It appears that these four beginning and veteran teachers think that students must be actively working on the "stuff." It is a view held by many other beginning and experienced teachers in the study. Classroom learning conditions, when right, enable students to work on acquiring new concepts, skills, or meanings. At first sight this finding seems obvious if not commonplace, but its implications are not. From the critical perspective of many, but not all, of this sample of young and older teachers, real teaching involves students' active engagement in critical modes of thought. Sizer's (Coalition of Essential Schools, 1991) "student as worker" metaphor (p. 226) in the classroom seems the most felicitous way to describe these beginners' and veterans' view of the classroom teaching and learning process. However, how this view of the classroom plays out in practice in varied school contexts is, of course, quite different, and is not necessarily bound to the other tenets of Sizer's educational reform movement, which emphasize a core curriculum, mastery of the subject matter by student exhibition, and a restructured school day (see Coalition of Essential Schools, 1991). (In fact, only one of these four teachers has had any contact or involvement with Sizer's Coalition of Essential Schools.) What, then, seems most critical is that these inexperienced and experienced teachers see "hard work" of students at the core of a successful class, and "fun" or "enthusiasm" as a correlative or derivative attribute of a challenging learning experience. A second-year suburban social studies teacher summed it up best.

> When I get people thinking and talking who don't often think and talk in my class. When I feel like the kids are engaged in the material, it is somehow meaningful to them in some way—interested in it. When I seem to reach more of the kids rather than a few of them. When the class is under control. When kids walk out of the class talking about what we have talked about—that's a good class.

The criteria of work, active engagement, and enjoyment on the part of students are not held by all of the young or older teachers in the study. Another view of a successful class is expressed by this rural school social studies teacher: "That kids are getting my message or my objectives; that kids are with me; that we don't have a lot of discipline hassles; that kids aren't bored." This more traditional view of teaching may be a reflection of the young teacher's philosophy or that she is in the first stage of development as a teacher, or both. Fuller (1969) and Burden (1981) both propose stages that educators go through as they develop as teachers. Both researchers claim that there are three stages: a beginning stage of survival focused on keeping one's head above water, a second stage of consolidation centering on mastery and refinement of basic teaching activities, and a final stage of mastery. It is not until the third stage that the teacher's main concern focuses on the students as learners and the teacher can see the overall pattern and needs of the learners. The beginning teachers in this study, including the new social studies teacher with her more traditional view of classroom teaching, do not fit neatly into the hierarchical developmental scheme of these researchers. On bad days they do. On good days they clearly don't. On most days? That is an open question and varies according to the teacher's teaching skill and circumstances. Rather than the posited developmental sequence, a nurturing school context or its opposite is likely to play a larger role in the professional development of these beginners. The goal, and the task, is, then, to provide beginning teachers with the enabling conditions and opportunities to experience more successes based on their criteria of a good class for learners and themselves.

To determine what factors teachers took into account when monitoring their teaching effectiveness, I used a variation of a two-part question that Lortie (1975) asked in his study of teachers. My question and possible responses were as follows:

> How do you gauge the effectiveness of your teaching—which of the following are you most likely to rely on as an indicator?
> 1. The reactions of other teachers who are familiar with my work and my students
> 2. The opinions expressed by students generally
> 3. My general observation of students in light of my views of what should be learned
> 4. The assessments made by the principal
> 5. The assessments made by a special supervisor, i.e., department chair, etc.
> 6. The results of objective examinations and various other tests
> 7. The reactions of students' parents
> 8. Other: (please write in)

In Lortie's (1975) study 59.1% of the 6,000 teachers overall and 64% of the younger teachers selected the third response. In our spring survey of this research study, 59% of all the teachers selected the third alternative. However, 71% of the 21 beginning teachers and only 48% of the 25 experienced teachers who responded chose that indicator. The majority of the experienced teachers chose their colleagues (8%), special supervisor (8%), students (8%), examinations (8%), or other (all of them) (16%) as the principal sources they relied on to determine their effectiveness. Similar to results in Lortie's study, none of the other possible choices were selected by more than 20% of the total participants in the survey. The conclusion that Lortie draws from the data is valid for this study as well: "These teachers give assent to norms which reflect dependence on self rather than others and personally held rather than 'vertically authoritative' opinions" (pp. 74–75). However much they may share common criteria for determining a successful class, it is the individual young teacher who monitors and authenticates his or her own progress and classroom effectiveness. It is essentially an individualistic rather than a collegial view of assessment that has not changed over time, place, or circumstance.

Sense of Efficacy

In studying how beginning teachers rate their overall effectiveness, it is especially important to ascertain how they view their impact and success in working with marginal and difficult-to-handle students. According to Ashton and Webb (1986), a way to assess their perspective is to consider the beginning teachers' beliefs and feelings with regard to their ability to teach and their students' ability to learn. This construct has been termed by them and other researchers as the teacher's "sense of efficacy." In a Rand Corporation research study (Berman, McLaughlin, Bass, Pauly, & Zeller, 1977), which Ashton and Webb draw upon, a teacher's sense of efficacy is defined as "the extent to which the teacher believed he or she had the capacity to affect student performance" (p. 137). The Rand research staff measured sense of efficacy by compiling the total scores from two Likert-scale items.

> When it comes right down to it, a teacher really can't do much because most of a student's motivation and performance depends on his or her home environment.

> If I really try hard, I can get through to even the most difficult or unmotivated students. (pp. 136–137)

The first item provides an indication of a teacher's general view: how effective the teaching profession can be in reaching all students (teaching efficacy). The second item gauges the teacher's perception of his or her competence to reach the students he or she actually teaches (personal efficacy). According to Ashton and Webb (1986), the two constructs are not correlated and, therefore, must be viewed as separate dimensions of the larger concept.[1]

---

1. Scoring is determined in the following manner: A total score of 8 or more indicates that a teacher has a high sense of efficacy; a score of 5 to 7 places the teacher in the moderate range, and 4 or less suggests the individual teacher has a low sense of efficacy to teach the most difficult students. In scoring each of the two constructs, sense of teaching efficacy and sense of personal efficacy, a different scale is used: 4 to 5 indicates high efficacy, 3 suggests moderate efficacy, and 1 to 2 implies low efficacy (Ashton & Webb, 1986).

These two Rand survey items were part of the questionnaires admin-istered to teachers in the fall and spring surveys. Table 6.1 shows the per-centage of beginning, veteran, and cooperating teachers who have a high, moderate, or low teaching or personal sense of efficacy. Looking first at the breakdown of the 38 beginning teachers who completed the questions in the fall survey, as anticipated at the start of the academic year a majority of new teachers have a positive view that all students can be motivated to learn. However, an appreciable number of novices had a belief that they could not reach all their students, regardless of how hard they tried.

As beginning teachers gain experience working with unmotivated and hard-to-teach adolescents, what happens to their sense of personal efficacy? How do the group's perceptions change over time? As indicated by the personal efficacy ratings of the 21 novices who responded to this item in both the fall and spring surveys, the trend is not encouraging. In the spring there is almost a 50–50 split between those teachers who hold a high and a low efficacy belief. Perhaps the trend is reflective of the norms of the school or of teachers with whom they have come in contact during their preparation or on the job. The beginners' scores can be compared with the sense-of-personal-efficacy scores of 14 veteran teachers who teach in the same schools as the beginning teachers. Also shown are the personal-efficacy results obtained in the spring survey for the experienced teachers as well as the 11 cooperating teachers.

The comparison suggests that more is at work than the school norms, colleagues' attitudes, or attitudes of cooperating teachers, some of whom served as supervisors during student teaching. This tentative and inconclu-

Table 6.1. Sense of Efficacy of Beginning, Veteran, and
Cooperating Teachers by Percentage

Type of Efficacy	Degree of Efficacy		
	High	Moderate	Low
Beginners, Fall 1988			
Teaching	57	24	19
Personal	57	5	38
Composite	46	43	11
Personal, Beginners			
Fall 1988	67	5	28
Spring 1989	47.5	5	47.5
Personal, Spring 1989			
Veteran	50	29	21
Veteran & Cooperating			
Teachers	60	20	20

served as supervisors during student teaching. This tentative and inconclusive finding indicates that the nature of the first-year teaching experience itself may lead to a diminution in the sense of personal efficacy of a number of the novices. Of course, this change of attitude may be a temporary phenomenon. As some of these beginners get on top of teaching and relate more effectively with "unmotivated" students, their disposition may once again reflect a greater sense of efficacy and empowerment. But the opposite is as likely to be true. Their disillusionment may harden into despair and frustration, leading to a "sense of learned helplessness" to affect positively—to use Jefferson's phrase—the "hearts and minds" of their "disaffected" or hard-to-reach students. This distinct possibility poses a dilemma for the profession.

Ashton and Webb's (1986) research indicated that a teacher's sense of personal efficacy may have real consequences in terms of how the teacher behaves toward these "low ability," or perhaps more accurately "low motivated," students and how these students perform academically. They state:

> Teachers with a strong sense of efficacy tended to have a classroom climate that is warm and supportive of student needs. Their students tended to feel secure and accepted and they scored higher on achievement tests than did the students of teachers with a lower sense of efficacy. (p. 144)

The implication is clear for teachers who adopt the lower sense-of-efficacy belief system: It portends the continuation of the "blaming the victim" cycle that has disempowered both teachers and their students.

The causes of a lower sense of efficacy are, of course, multifaceted and complex. Ashton and Webb (1986) cite such psychosocial conditions as "isolation of teachers, their uncertainty, their lack of support and recognition and their sense of powerlessness and alienation" (p. 159). It clearly varies. My view is that two of the more important factors at work for those beginning teachers who have changed from a high sense of personal efficacy to a lower sense of personal competence are a sense of failure and a conflict of values with these students about the nature of work and learning in the classroom. A first-year and a second-year teacher make the points poignantly.

First-Year Rural English Teacher

I'd just got through one period, and they were just unruly that day. I remember just sitting down at my desk—we have four or five minutes between classes, which gives you a long time to just wait for your next class. I'm thinking, "What am I doing here? I'm not doing anything for these kids, these kids are not learning anything." That's almost the most disheartening thing for a first-year teacher—that you're giving something to them, and that they have to be learning something. If you're not, then you feel like, why bother? I shouldn't even be here. It was the worst.

Second-Year Suburban Social Studies Teacher
I am the classic overachiever-perfectionist, and it was really hard to fail. Also I don't like being treated lousily, and you are often treated as the "teacher," an object. You're treated really badly, and that hurts for a long time. They pulled stuff because of my age. They would try to ask me questions like, "Do you smoke pot? Have you had sex?" We're talking about a standard track class—a few of those kids have dropped out, many have been left back. It's a particularly tough class but it's a tough level anyway.

Sarason's (1971) view of teaching helps give perspective to the remarks of these two beginning teachers. In *The Culture of School and the Problem of Change*, he makes clear both the difficulty and the reciprocal nature of teaching.

> Constant giving in the context of constant vigilance required by the presence of many children is a demanding, draining, taxing affair that cannot be easily sustained. . . . To sustain the giving at a high level required that the teacher experience getting. The sources for getting are surprisingly infrequent and indirect. (p. 167)

Probably, many first-year teachers will experience initial failure in relating to the difficult-to-handle adolescent. There will be no mutuality—the teacher will give but will not often receive positive feedback from these students. Failing often will, of course, make the teacher question his or her personal sense of efficacy. Being hurt and offended by some of these students does not help matters for young, middle-class professionals who have not often faced rejection and nonacceptance.

In addition, many of these students do not share the "hard work" ethic of these beginning teachers. An ethnographic study of a British secondary school (Woods, 1978) revealed a pattern of beliefs that also holds for many low-achieving American adolescents.

> To these pupils at least, it is not the work that is important, and any intrinsic satisfaction to be had from it is dependent on the relationship with the teachers concerned. This squares with their general emphasis on social criteria in their outlook on schools. (p. 167)

    Until the teacher is tested, liked, and accepted by these students, no efficacious working relationship will be established in the classroom. It follows that without such a relationship the teacher's sense of personal efficacy to make a difference will be lessened, if not permanently diminished. Given the way many public schools are presently constituted, teachers can survive, but not flourish, in these "tough" classrooms by resorting to the kind of compromises Sizer (1984) details in *Horace's Compromise*: lower one's expectations, give busy work, and don't require too much hard work or active engagement in learning. For many beginning teachers in this study these compromises are diametrically opposed to their criteria for good teaching. The dilemma for the profession is how to prevent this state of affairs from happening in the classrooms of beginning teachers, so that their sense of personal efficacy and their effectiveness as teachers will not be undermined. An inservice workshop will not do. Instead, it requires the collective wisdom and the sustained effort of teacher educators, school administrators, and particularly those veteran teachers within the school who possess a high sense of personal efficacy. These professionals need to work with and support new teachers in ways that enable the newcomers to the profession to reach the adolescents most at risk. It is a formidable task — difficult but doable. However, the school norms and the prevailing "sink or swim" view of learning to teach in many schools will have to change faster than they presently are evolving.

CHAPTER 7

Problems of Classroom Management

When asked about the first major crisis encountered in the classroom, one first-year teacher responded:

> My first major crisis? Second period is a major crisis once a week. It's a class of 20 and there's five of them that absolutely do not care. They don't care if they fail, they don't care if they turn the work in to you, they don't care if they get sent out of the room, they don't care if they get detention. I was really shocked at some of the kids who will just say, "This class sucks" to your face, or "You don't care," or "You're just picking on me" in front of the rest of the class.

This chapter discusses the major problems and dilemmas beginning teachers encounter in their everyday teaching. The data are drawn from the fall and spring surveys and from interviews with 21 of the 38 beginners. When appropriate, veteran teachers' responses to survey questions are also included to provide comparison and context in analyzing the substantive problems and issues that confront teachers in schools. The first section details the general problems beginners perceive in teaching. In the second section the substantive focus is on the principal issue many beginners face: the testing of their classroom authority.

PROBLEMS IN TEACHING

Teachers' Perceptions

Both first- and second-year teachers and the veteran teachers surveyed were asked to list the three most serious problems they faced in their teaching. Table 7.1 shows the top 12 problems in terms of frequency of response of the beginning teachers and the veteran teachers who participated in the study. The rankings are not based on a random sample, but they are useful

Table 7.1. Ranking of Problems in Teaching by Teachers in Survey Sample

Problems	Beginners		Veterans	
	Rank of problem	% citing most serious	Rank of problem	% citing most serious
Classroom discipline	1	48	2.5	29
Student motivation	2	43	1	62
Curriculum	3	38	2.5	29
Planning of lessons	4	24		0
Relations with students	5	24	4	25
Heavy workload	6	13	7.5	12
Job stress	7	13	12	8
Lack of time	8	12	6	16
Grading & assessment	9	11		0
Clerical/hall duties	10	8		0
Relations with colleagues	11	8	7.5	12
Relations with parents	12	2	5	16

nevertheless in suggesting the areas of greatest concern of inexperienced and experienced teachers.

While the two lists differ, it is clear that the top two problems of the beginning teachers are quite similar to those of the veteran teachers and center on the issues of classroom power and authority and students' attitude toward learning and academic achievement. At first sight there may appear to be an appreciable difference between beginners and veterans in regard to their perceptions of the seriousness of classroom discipline versus student lack of motivation. If, however, these problems are viewed as interrelated, the distinction disappears. That is, classroom discipline/student motivation are viewed by 91% of the beginners and 91% of the veterans as their most serious ongoing dual concern. One would, of course, anticipate that classroom discipline would be a more serious problem for the new teacher than for an experienced classroom teacher, but the fact that almost 30% of veteran teachers rank it a problem suggests that it may also manifest itself in other ways, such as a lack of motivation or effort. Furthermore, establishing and maintaining legitimate classroom authority while helping students make academic progress are the principal tasks of any classroom teacher. It is, therefore, not surprising that the perceived problems of beginning teachers and veteran teachers correspond so closely. Finally, classroom discipline may also be more of a problem in some schools than in others. As one first-year teacher in a rural school put it, "My main problems are with discipline, but every other teacher here has problems with it. I think it's particularly bad in this school."

These tentative findings also support the supposition that the beginning teachers' problems cannot be viewed in isolation or regarded only as "rookie problems" that, like acne in adolescence, will go away with time. Student compliance and students' achievement and motivation are ongoing concerns of young and older teachers, as reflected in informal conversations with them as well as in periodic surveys of their common problems (Dunn, 1972; Pharr, 1974).

However, the younger and the more experienced teachers perceive the interrelated problems of student motivation and classroom discipline in substantially different ways. Here are the responses of a young and an older English teacher who work at the same school and teach at the same junior-high grade levels. The beginning teacher cites "students who are unmotivated" and "inexperience in terms of classroom discipline" as two of her most serious problems. The veteran English teacher remarks that her two most serious problems are "student emotional problems due to abuse or neglect by parents" and "parent apathy—parents who refuse to cooperate or even engage in dialogue about their own children's work in school." While the beginning teacher seemingly focuses on the more immediate and surface manifestations of the problem of reaching and controlling young adolescents in her classes, the veteran teacher emphasizes the underlying causes that lead to some of her students' inappropriate classroom behavior.

These two perceptions of the same classroom phenomenon appear at first glance to be distinctly different. But is it a distinction that, in fact, makes a difference in how a teacher during a class thinks about the problem and how she may act to resolve or manage the problem? In this particular case, the young teacher's thinking about the problem—that it is her inexperience that causes her classroom discipline problems—may lead her to focus only on acquiring better classroom management techniques, basically a "band-aid" approach. But her more experienced colleague—a 15-year veteran—may also be forced to employ the same ad hoc strategy because of her perceived inability to address the underlying problems of the situation, even though she is seemingly more aware of the limited value and lack of long-term effectiveness of the strategy. There is, of course, another interpretation of the veteran teacher's thinking. Some school critics would argue that the experienced teacher's analysis of the underlying causes of students' poor classroom performance may be an attempt to justify her failure to reach or teach these troubled and often difficult-to-handle adolescents.

Berliner's (1988) studies on pedagogical expertise have focused on the developmental differences between the "expert and the novice teacher." He contends that "those in the early stages of the development of skill in pedagogy do not use the same frameworks for interpreting classroom information as those in later stages" (p. 21). Inexperienced teachers often "lack organizing frameworks or complete classroom schemata for interpreting classroom information," which results in their having difficulty distinguishing the "forest and the trees" (p. 20). While there is some degree of truth to his remarks, it might not be a lack of cognitive frameworks or lack of cognitive sophistication to evaluate classroom life that leads the beginning teachers in this study to view their discipline problems in an "unsophisticated" light. These beginners, like the four teachers described in the case studies, have substantive training in the liberal arts that prepares them well to analyze and evaluate complex phenomena. Indeed, in my interviews, they were often able to discuss cogently the underlying causes of the classroom discipline problems many of them faced.

While there are not sufficient hard data in the study to challenge seriously Berliner's thesis, Elizabeth Alberto's case study is instructive and provides a counter example that at least suggests that these general conclusions may need to be qualified. She has expertise and working knowledge in foreign-language oral proficiency in the classroom that is superior to most if not all of her colleagues in a leading public school foreign-language department. Her expertise in both content and pedagogy suggests that not all beginning teachers lack cognitive frameworks or sophistication in substantive aspects of classroom teaching of subject matter. Computer "whiz kids" at colleges and universities in the 1970s and 1980s often had greater understanding and insight into computer programming than many of their professors. Bernard Bailyn (1960) in his groundbreaking work, *Education in the Forming of American Society*, makes a similar point about early colonists who confronted the first frontier of the Atlantic coast. He writes:

> To all of the settlers the wilderness was strange and forbidding, full of unexpected problems and enervating hardships. To none was there available reliable lore or reserves of knowledge and experience to draw upon in gaining control over the environment: parents no less than children faced the world afresh. In terms of mere effectiveness, in fact, the young — less bound by prescriptive memories, more adaptable, more vigorous — stood often at advantage. Learning faster, they came to see the world more familiarly, to concede more readily to unexpected necessities, to sense more accurately the phasing of a new life. They and not their parents became the effective guides to a new world. (p. 22)

In terms of educational innovation — at the frontiers of knowledge — it is often the younger rather than the experienced teacher who is the principal inquirer who initially distinguishes the forest from the trees. Berliner's views of the expert teacher may hold in normal times and under standard conditions. But at times of experimentation and uncertainty the novice teacher may be the "wiser head."

Rather than a lack of cognitive sophistication, the real reason that some able beginning teachers have difficulty in the classroom may have to do with lack of both practice with a particular teaching or classroom management strategy and reflection about their teaching. That these neophyte teachers are not more reflective is probably the result of a combination of factors: the "indeterminate," "highly contextual," and "frenetically paced" nature of classroom teaching (Zeichner, 1983); the limited value of theory in informing daily classroom practice (McDonald, 1986); and insufficient time during and after a stressful school day for the new teacher to pause, deliberate, and plan carefully for the next day or next week. High school teaching is often "teaching on the run." It is that way for the neophyte, and it is often that way for the veteran teacher with 20 or more years of experience. As one first-year teacher remarked, "It feels like a rollercoaster—not exactly knowing what's around the corner and all of a sudden you're there in terms of midterms or different events around the school." In these circumstances, there may be at best what Schön (1987) terms "reflection-in-action," or on-the-spot classroom problem solving and experimentation (p. 26). There is little time or energy left for systematic or deeper "reflection-on-action," particularly of the variety involving "theory building" or the application of theory to practice in the real and messy world of the beginning teacher's classroom.

There is perhaps one other substantive reason that many teachers do not seriously evaluate their teaching. It is the fact that few in education really value reflection. This attitude is, of course, embedded in the "hidden curriculum" of the schools, the schools of education, and the larger society. While lip service is often given to the need for self-assessment and the measurement of professional and personal growth, many teachers and school administrators do not see the value in self-reflection. It is not sufficiently encouraged in preparation programs or in inservice education. Instead, there is ingrained in many teachers the need to be "doers" and persons-of-action. Just as most schools and most other American institutions "muddle through," many American teachers also practice the art of the possible in the context of present and immediate realities.

Degree of Seriousness

In an international study analyzing the research findings on beginning teachers' problems in North America, Europe, Australia, and New Zealand, the Dutch scholar Simon Veenman (1984) lists the 24 most frequent problems that novice teachers report they encounter in their initial years of teaching. Veenman's meta-analysis focused on the findings of 83 studies, including 55 research projects in the United States, that were conducted between 1960 and 1984. The top five concerns of beginning teachers were classroom discipline, motivating students, dealing with individual students, relations with parents, and assessing student work. The first two problems of Veenman's large sample match the top concerns of the beginning teachers and veteran teachers of this study. One of the other three problems, dealing with individual students, is also a high priority of both beginning and veteran teachers in the beginning-teacher sample of classroom teachers. Relations with parents and assessing student work, while certainly serious problems for some, are of secondary concern, particularly for the majority of the younger teachers in the survey.

To determine more precisely the seriousness of the problems that the beginning teachers confronted, first- and second-year teachers in this sample were asked to rate the degree of seriousness of each of the 24 problems Veenman listed in his research review.[1] (Veenman's meta-study includes as beginning teachers both first- and second-year teachers. The majority of the individual beginners' studies he analyzed, however, focused on first-year teachers.) Table 7.2 details how the novice teachers as a whole rated the degree of seriousness of these common teaching problems as opposed to the frequency of problems that Table 7.1 displays. Perhaps the most interesting finding is that except for one item, "lack of spare time," the majority of both first- and second-year teachers rated all the remaining problems as mildly serious or not at all serious. (In fact, no beginner rated 17 of these particular problems as extremely serious, and for eight of the 17, no one rated the problems as either very serious or extremely serious.) In addition to the time pressure issue the newcomers faced, the five other most significant concerns of the group as a whole were "dealing with individual differences in the classroom"; "motivating students"; "dealing with slow learners"; "dealing with problems of individual students"; and "classroom discipline." Only on two items did the majority of first-year and second-year teachers differ substantially: 54% of first-year teachers considered motivating students a serious problem, compared with 17% of second-year teachers; 50% of first-year teachers but only 17% of second-year teachers regarded dealing with slow learners a serious problem. From these data, it can be inferred that by the start of the second year of teaching, many beginning teachers feel they have achieved a greater sense of efficacy and acquired a set of teaching strategies and procedures that allow them

---

1. The beginners were asked to rate the seriousness of the problem on a five-point Likert scale ("not at all serious," "mildly serious," "moderately serious," "very serious," and "extremely serious"). In tabulating the results, these categories were collapsed to "less serious" (for the first two categories) and "more serious" problems (for the last three categories).

Table 7.2. Seriousness of Beginning Teachers' Problems: Comparison of Survey Sample and International Study

	Survey Sample			International
		% indicating		
Problems	Rank of problem	Less serious	More serious	rank of problem
1. Lack of spare time	1	42	58	22
2. Dealing with individual differences in classroom	2	55	45	3
3. Motivating students	3	58	42	2
4. Dealing with slow learners	4	61	39	9
5. Dealing withproblems of individual students	5	61	39	
6. Classroom discipline	6	68	32	1
7. Determining learning level of students	7	68	32	14
8. Heavy teaching load resulting in insufficient preparation time	8	68	32	9
9. Insufficient materials & supplies	9	71	29	7
10.Effective use of different teaching methods	10	74	26	12
11.Organization of class time & activities	11	74	26	6
12.Burden of clerical work	12	74	26	16
13.Effective use of textbooks & clerical guides	13	79	21	21
14.Dealing with students of different cultures & deprived backgrounds	14	82	18	20
15.Knowledge of subject matter	15	82	18	15
16.Assessing student work	16	84	16	4
17.Inadequate guidance & support	17	86	14	11
18.Planning of lessons & school day	18	87	13	11
19.Relations with parents	19	87	13	5
20.Awareness of school policies	20	89	11	13
21.Inadequate equipment	21	89	11	18
22.Large class size	22	92	8	24
23.Relations with colleagues	23	97	3	10
24.Relations with principal/ administrators	24	100	0	17

to teach the more difficult-to-handle students in their schools more effectively.

The data taken as a whole suggest that the major problems of teaching are perceived by the beginning teachers as manageable and part of the normal routine of daily teaching. In their views, the more serious problems center on teaching and motivating the more difficult students—the slow learners or the troubled students. A second set of problems that appear to be mildly serious in nature cluster around general classroom practices: "determining learning levels of students"; "insufficient materials and supplies"; "effective use of different teaching methods"; "organization of class time and activities"; "effective use of textbooks and clerical guides"; and "assessing student work." Among the least serious, if not negligible, problems are those relating to professional relations with parents, teachers, and school administrators. For example, a majority indicated as not at all serious "relations with parents" (57%); "relations with colleagues" (76%); and "relations with principal/administrators" (86%).

While these findings are, of course, far from definitive, they do suggest that the phenomenon of "reality shock" may not be as serious or debilitating as some researchers and the folk traditions of our craft often purport. Reality shock, while never adequately defined, refers to the initial cultural shock of first-year teaching in which a naive and often idealistic beginner faces the "harsh and rude reality of everyday teaching" (Veenman, 1984, p. 143). In this sense, few, if any, of the 38 first- or second-year teachers underwent a series of dramatic and traumatic experiences, losing in the process their idealism while they adopted the more traditional and custodial role of the classroom teacher. Rather, they seemed to indicate that they knew what they were in for from the start, and may even have been surprised at how well they were adapting to their new role. There were, of course, exceptions. One suburban social studies teacher put it this way: "I no longer want to 'save the world,' just teach decent kids and enjoy myself a little in the process." But a more typical response was that of another first-year teacher who said, "I love it! It is what I expected but it isn't always easy."

Classroom Crises

Reality shock also refers to the longer-term "assimilation of complex reality which forces itself incessantly upon the beginning teacher, day-in and day-out" (Veenman, 1984, p. 143). In this sense, the majority of beginning teachers did confront and actively deal with the interrelated web of problems of the classroom, the school, and the community. These complex and often difficult-to-handle problems are revealed in the reflections of many of the 19 teachers who were observed and interviewed. When asked to describe their first major crisis or most difficult problem as a teacher, these first- or second-year teachers often told poignant stories that reveal the full complexity and often perplexity of beginning teaching. The "tough" problems selected center on classroom control and authority.

A second-year teacher in a wealthy suburban school reflects about the major problem he confronted during his first year of teaching.

> The kid had a behavioral problem—hyperactive and on medication. I tried to keep him under control. One day he stormed out of class and swore at me. My biggest problem immediately was re-establishing my relationship with the class. I thought I had to do something to regain their respect. I felt my authority was threatened. How do I control that situation? How do I deal with him, and how do I deal with the class who witness this occurrence? I don't deal well with being an authority figure. I'm not a strict disciplinarian. I try to argue more through reason and that doesn't always work with high school kids who sometimes are just impervious to reason. Later, there was another kid in the same class who swore at me in class, and it became a power issue—which I hate.
>
> Those types of issues are most painful for me. I haven't developed a very comfortable disciplinarian approach. I am strict on certain things like tardiness and skipping class. But as far as discipline and their behavior, it is harder for me to do. That's something about my personality.

A second-year social studies teacher at a school whose town is changing from a rural to a more suburban community discusses a crisis that occurred during the initial year of teaching.

> In one class there was a black student who I got along with very well. In this school there are very few black kids. But he was much older; he was 17 or 18 years old, from LA, a sort of tough kid, a bit of a leader with the rest of the kids. The way I handled him was to give him a little bit of power in the classroom so that he would be more responsible. It was a mistake; he took it as being in control of the classroom. It wasn't an immediate crisis. But it was something that built and built, until he was singing rap songs in class that had lyrics that you shouldn't say in public. He'd sing these lyrics as he was walking out the door; but I'd just catch it; I mean real foul language. Personally, we were fine. He would love to come in and do things for me; he moved my desk for me, a real heavy desk; there was no problem. But he was just a teenager who had been living in California

and back here. He had gone back and forth, a real troubled home situation.

Because of the last thing he did, I kicked him out of the class. And as he walked out, he said to me, "You're pushing it, lady." I wasn't afraid of him—he was a real pain in the butt—but he wasn't going to hurt me. However, I felt I should tell my superior. I told the head of the department, and he moved on it. There is a real underlying feeling of racism in the school—there was a little bit of "big black kid threatening a white teacher"—which I didn't feel. But he was threatening, which is not allowed—whether he meant it or not. Boom! The kid's out of my class. He's suspended for two weeks. His aunt, I think, in whose home he's staying, came in because she was afraid it was an incident of racism. And we had a talk; she was fine when I told her my experience. She said, "That's my [nephew] being my [nephew]. What you did was fine. You should have been tougher on him."

A first-year female minority teacher in a large urban school related this incident.

One day a student walked in that didn't belong in my classroom—somewhere around the second or third month of classes. He walked to the back of the room as if I wasn't there, and started talking to his girlfriend who was back there. And I said, "Excuse me, please. Let me have your program card. Would you mind telling me what are you doing here?" He just ignored me. He just continued talking. And I asked him to please let me have his program card, which is like an I.D. He refused and said, "Get out of my way!" And I said, "You are not leaving this room until you give me your program card." He turned around and spoke to his girlfriend in a very cold, chilled tone: "Come and take care of this bitch for me." I said, "Look, you are not leaving here until you give me your program card." His girlfriend came across the room and said "Ms. [X], he just came to give me something." And I said, "I know this is not the way you behave." He said to her again, "I told you to smack this bitch for me." At this point I figured, well, let him go, because I don't want any scene to happen here in this classroom—this was the class that I was having problems with already. So I let him go, and then tried to get her to give me his name and stuff. So far we have been watching out for him to this day. He has never been back, and she has never been back to school either. They knew they did something wrong. And it was pretty scary. I mean it gave me chills on my spine. That was as bad as it has gotten.

A first-year mathematics teacher in another rural New England school relates the first, and at this point only, confrontation with an angry parent of a middle school child.

It was my only real crisis so far. One day after school, I was just going about my business, and a woman came in and started yelling at me because I had given her son two detentions that day. One detention was for not having anything to write with, and one detention was for not having anything to write on. I had to do this because they'll come to class without anything. So all he had was his book, and she came in and she said, "Do you mean to tell me that you have given him two detentions because he didn't have a pencil and paper?" And I said, "Yes, it's true." She said, "Well, I don't know why he didn't have a pencil but this school provides paper to the students." And I said, "That's true but . . . ," and she wouldn't let me get in a word edgewise. She wouldn't let me speak. The argument that I wanted to make was, "I would have provided him paper but he never asked; the time to get the paper is before school." This is the stuff I wanted to say, "I don't care where he gets his paper, I'll give him all the paper he wants as long as he has it when he needs it so time is not wasted in the class." She wouldn't let me say any of that. Instead, she started telling me that I wasn't qualified to teach him, that I didn't like him, and that I was prejudiced against him and that he's never learned anything from my class or any other class. In fact, the whole school system was terrible and that she was going to yank him out of the school system.

Of course, I was getting very frustrated and angry because I couldn't even defend myself. We went down to the principal's office because I knew that's where it had to go. By the end of that meeting, I was so frustrated that I was bawling my eyes out. I was just crying. It wasn't because I felt that I was wrong, and it wasn't because I felt like I was beaten by this woman, I was just so frustrated and tired of everything.

Classroom teaching is often depicted as routine and predictable. These accounts, however, demonstrate the uncertainty and, in Dewey's (1938) terms, the "problematic" nature of classroom teaching. Doyle (1977), too, speaks of the "multidimensionality, simultaneity and unpredictability of the classroom environment" (p. 55). Each of these "crises" dealing with classroom practice is open-ended. There is no one neat solution to control "acting out" students, to deal with a hostile youngster who enters your class without permission, to handle a troubled minority student in a white school environment, or to have an angry and upset parent hear you out and accept the rationale for your disciplinary action.

These "war stories" raise as many questions as they answer about the rookie experiences of these bright and articulate beginning teachers. What rookie mistakes were made? What theoretical perspectives should inform practice in these cases? What "craft wisdom" or practical knowledge needs to be imparted to the beginner to avoid or reduce the level of conflict and tension inherent in these problematic situations? Can the beginning teacher become more reflective and more effective in dealing with these "realities" of secondary classroom teaching? Thoughtful scholars and veteran practitioners may well disagree on the correct answers to these questions or even on the decision-making process to follow in coming to closure on these tough classroom teaching issues that confront the novice teacher. But it is also clear that these problems of classroom practice require deeper thought and wider dialogue.

TESTING OF CLASSROOM AUTHORITY

A common thread running through those classroom conflicts is the testing of the beginning teacher's leadership authority. There are at least three dimensions of the problem: where to "draw the line" with students so that classroom control and productive learning may be maintained; the process by which a teacher's authority is recognized and accepted by students and parents, teachers and administrators; and the new teacher's personal and professional view of his or her role as an authority figure in the classroom.

Drawing the Line

As the above critical incidents illustrate, the most problematic task of the beginning teacher relates to drawing the line with students so that classroom deportment and control are maintained. The process involves more than the teacher simply making clear his or her set of classroom expectations. In fact, almost all the new teachers do exactly that on the first day of teaching. Following the advice of veteran teachers, department heads, or their former college supervisors, many of them handed out a list of the "dos and don'ts" that were designed to alert and inform students about appropriate classroom conduct. The tougher problem, of course, is following through daily in enforcing the rules in a flexible but consistent manner that also matches the school norms held by students, teachers, and administrators. As can be seen in the examples, a teacher can be too wishy-washy or even too strict and literal about enforcing the "bottom line." Teachers can violate school norms by giving up some of their authority or can place themselves in a precarious situation by asserting authority without the power to enforce the command. "Learning the ropes" in terms of negotiating life in the classroom and school involves for these beginners much trial-and-error learning, perhaps in certain cases even "trial by ordeal."

In managing classroom life, there is the problem of dealing with uncertainty, of having to make an "on the spot" decision without clear reference to a set of standard procedures. Many of the problem situations reveal so graphically the dilemmas that can occur that are totally unexpected but demand almost immediate action. As Floden and Clark (1988) assert, "uncertainty is especially troubling for novice teachers" (p. 505). They have as yet no anchor or compass to navigate troubled waters. Yet, dealing with unexpected dilemmas is part of the teacher's professional life. They won't go away with time. Lampert (1985) refers to teachers as "dilemma managers," an appropriate phrase to describe the highly complex work of the secondary teacher (p. 190). Helping novice teachers cope with serious dilemmas requires more sophisticated preprofessional training as well as more effective inservice training than presently exists in higher education or in the secondary schools. But Schön (1987) quotes a dean of a prestigious business school who laments, "We need most to teach students how to make decisions under conditions of uncertainty, but that is just what we don't know how to teach" (p. 4). The statement holds true for schools of education as well. Until the schools of education and the profession itself get a better grip on the "problem," it is at least important to convey to newcomers the practical advice of this first-year teacher: "Be willing to tackle anything that might happen; some things are unexpected on any given day."

Acceptance of the Teacher's Authority

For the beginning teacher whose professional identity is still being molded, the problem of recognition and acceptance as a "real" teacher can be particularly difficult. In his discussion of identity formation, Erikson (1968) makes clear that before one's identity is fully achieved the "psychosocial reciprocity" of the community of significant others is necessary. In the eyes of those who matter—parents, teachers, and peers—the individual must appear to be what he or she professes. There must result "mutual affirmation" (p. 219). It is also reasonable to assume that a teacher's professional identity is in part dependent on the acknowledgment by significant others in the school community that the newcomer is regarded as a full-fledged teacher. In the secondary school context, this means students, their parents, and other teachers and supervisors taking the new teacher seriously and according the neophyte appropriate respect as an authority who is in control of both the classroom and the content.

In the spring survey, the beginners were asked to indicate what time (month) in the academic year they "felt really accepted" by the principal, other teachers, and students. For the most part, the beginning teachers felt that students, administrators, and their colleagues accepted them as "real

Figure 7.1. Beginning Teachers' Acceptance by Others

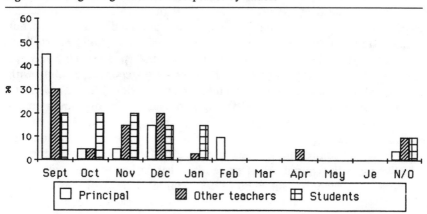

teachers" by the end of the first five months of teaching.[2] As Figure 7.1 illustrates, of the 21 new teachers who responded to the second questionnaire in May, a majority felt students had fully accepted them as "the teacher" by the Thanksgiving holiday. The pattern for acceptance by teachers and school administrators is similar, except that nine (45%) of the beginning teachers in the sample cited September as the time their principals really accepted them as professionals. However, another four (19%) teachers perceived that they still had not been accepted by their principals in June. Interestingly, no group of significant others accepted the beginners in March, May, or June, and only one teacher indicated he was accepted by his faculty in April.

These survey results suggest that school/community acceptance of the beginning teacher may not be immediate or automatic. For many, it is acquired over time, and for some it is not granted. There is a crucial difference, Weber (1958) points out in his important work on modern bureaucracy, between positional and personal authority. On accepting the job, positional authority is bestowed upon the teacher by the institution. Personal authority develops and evolves from the personality and competence of the teacher; it is conferred by students only when, in their eyes, it is earned. When the neophyte teacher is not fully accepted by significant

---

2. Since most of the new teachers' contact with parents was minimal and infrequent, it was not possible in this study to gauge how teachers felt about parents' acceptance of them as the "person in charge."

others in the school community, problems can occur, as in the case of the urban teacher who confronts an uninvited stranger in her class and of the middle school teacher who is forced to deal with an angry and defiant parent. In each of these cases, the teacher's authority is challenged, and the neophyte faces the possibility of loss of face as well as respect. However, over the course of the academic year, things are likely to improve. As a first-year teacher remarked, "When I got to know the students better and had earned their regard, teaching became easier. However, as for feeling like a legitimate classroom teacher, that will take a few more years."

While the testing of the teacher's authority will usually diminish with time as the newcomer becomes fully socialized in the role, this testing will never go away completely. All teachers in a contemporary secondary school confront students, parents, and even other teachers who question their authority. Students go to the department head or the principal, parents go over the heads of the teacher, even up to the superintendent and the school board. Other teachers file grievances against colleagues for violating the collective bargaining agreement, as one of the veteran teachers reported happened to him. Before the February vacation, he left school an hour earlier than normal to catch a flight to the Soviet Union. A team of his students was participating in an international debate with their Soviet counterparts, and their plane flight had to be rescheduled, forcing their departure before the end of the school day. He was reported. As this incident reveals, the surprising and the bizarre happen even to the most experienced and well-intentioned teachers in such complex organizations as the modern secondary school. Beginning teachers should at least be made aware by teacher educators and experienced teachers in their schools that their authority may be tested in unique ways as they learn their new role and even after they have mastered their craft.

Teacher as Authority Figure

A number of novices in their first year of teaching wrestle with defining or redefining their classroom persona as authority figures. It is both a personal and professional concern that goes beyond naiveté or inexperience in dealing with recalcitrant and unruly adolescents. At its core, it is a values issue that often relates to the individual's upbringing and emerging world view as a young middle- or upper middle-class adult. The white female teacher who works in a "blue collar" school and had the encounter with the black student put it this way.

The biggest dilemma to me was being an authority figure. I wasn't a troublemaker, but I was always sort of anti-authoritarian. I had a real hard time becoming a "They." I was always an "Us" and now I'm a "They." Because of this attitude, it made it hard to discipline. I was buying a little too much into the sixties stuff of sharing with the kids— that doesn't work in this school. With these kids, they just laugh at it. We had an assistant principal who was that way, and the students would say, "Oh, yeah, send me down to Dr. [X]. We'll share, we'll talk. Great, kick me out of class." So that obviously doesn't work too well. So I had a real conflict on how to deal with discipline because I didn't want to be too hard, and yet I heard myself say things like: "If you do that one more time . . . !" You can't believe you'd ever say that, and there I was having to say stuff like that.

It appears that this second-year teacher recognizes in the context of her school environment that a more strict disciplinary approach is necessary, if for no other reason than sheer survival. Likewise, the second-year teacher who works in a wealthy upper middle-class Boston suburb with over 90% of the students going on to college also has come to understand that reason and heart-to-heart discussion do not always work in his classes. But his general philosophy of classroom management based on Erasmian principles of tolerance, reason, and moral argument does work in most of his classes, most of the time, and particularly during his second year of teaching. As he states, "This year has not really been a problem. I have really good rapport with the kids and that creates an atmosphere of mutual respect in which any time they do get a little bit out of hand—usually it's the pressure from other classmates who immediately put it down."

On the fundamental level, the initial "problem" of these two teachers involves the exercise of power: the use of "commands," "threats," and "punishment" as instruments of control over their students—the very techniques of discipline they resented and abhorred as students themselves, and that were alien to their views of education when they started teaching. As the British philosopher Peters (1960) speculates, "It may well be that the ability to exercise power may be a necessary condition for the exercise of some forms of authority. Behind the voice there is often the cane" (p. 21). At least in their schools, the two teachers confronted and were forced to deal with this classroom reality in the first year of teaching.

In both cases, these teachers seem to reconcile the dilemma by either redefining their notion of discipline in the context of their school or their individual classes, or by working out a view of discipline that allows the use in their classes of either the strict disciplinary approach or the more permissive moral persuasion approach to classroom control. This pragmatic compromise is best summed up in the statement of a first-year teacher in a rural working-class community: "I don't like to be an a-hole, and my biggest dilemma was having to decide whether or not to be one in order to maintain discipline in the classroom. I found out I had to be one sometimes, but not always. However, I still dislike the role."

There is, of course, one other way to view the issue of power and authority in the classroom. A beginning teacher in an experimental school articulates this alternative viewpoint.

> What I'm trying to get to in my classroom is that they have power. I'm trying to allow students to have power—to know what their knowledge is and to learn to create their own ideas as opposed to my being the one who is the only holder of ideas in the universe. I want to transfer the authority back to them.

Because her comments reflect the prevailing view of this small, neo-progressive public school, she is able to implement her philosophy in her upper-level middle school classroom. Of course, she is being tested by her students just as other beginners are in other schools. But the structure of the school and the organization of the school day, which permits more personalization and more time with each class, are school variables that allow her a chance to succeed in redefining the authority relationships in her classes.

In his study of how beginning teachers adapt to differing school contexts, Lacey (1977), a British researcher, defines three ways of responding to school norms: category I, or "internalized adjustment," by which the beginning teacher generally accepts the prevailing institutional pattern of behavior as appropriate; category II, or "strategic compliance," which involves the novice adjusting his or her behavior in light of the school norms but still maintaining reservations; and category III, or "strategically redefining the situation," by which the new teacher actively works to change the current set of role expectations (pp. 72–73). While in this study the large majority of beginning teachers interviewed accept with little question the school norms as given, the four who are quoted earlier fit the second category—teachers who at least at the start of the school year only reluctantly comply with the "way things are." The data reveal no discernible pattern for their slight "deviance" from the norm. Two of these beginning teachers were male, and two were female; two were graduates of master's programs, and two received their teacher preparation at the undergraduate level. Two were social studies teachers, one an English teacher, and one a science teacher. All four of the novice teachers were in their early to mid-twenties. Two of the beginners in the sample of 19—the first-year and a second-year teacher in the experimental school—were working along with their principal and colleagues to change school and classroom norms significantly. Clearly, more research is needed to determine what personality and environmental factors are likely to produce American teachers who adopt "strategic compliance" as their way of coping with and questioning the realities of their school situation.

Depending on one's educational philosophy, the survey results may be encouraging or discouraging. The more reform-minded, progressive educator would desire some more category III teachers — change agents who question and work to change the status quo and the power relations within the classroom and school. The progressive presumably would also like to see many more category II skeptics who will, with time, see the need for change and systematic reform. Other educators of the clinical-supervision school would hope that these new teachers were a bit more reflective or at least had the opportunity to think about and converse with other professionals about the teaching dilemma and possible alternative action. The more conservative educator and the more radical educator of the critical-pedagogy school — for opposite reasons — would probably lament how some of these rookies were ill-equipped and ill-informed about the nature of power and authority in bureaucratic institutions that compel attendance of immature or resisting "clients." Still other practitioners of the craft might find some hope in the way that these new professionals thought about and handled the difficult classroom dilemmas in their initial year of teaching. It is not all bad that a neophyte's mettle is tested "under fire," and that the newcomer's values and views of human nature are exposed and examined in the real world of the classroom. Through such a process the beginner's idealism may be chastened, but over time his or her view of education may also become more sophisticated and refined by this form of decision making under pressure. After all, in Barr and Dreeben's (1980) phrase, this is the first time the first-year professional confronts the "hand the teacher is dealt" without the support of a cooperating teacher or college supervisor. In most risk-taking occupations, an individual can and does learn from experience. To quote Oliver Wendell Holmes, "A page of history is worth a volume of logic" (*New York Trust Co.* v. *Eisner*, 1921). This pragmatic aphorism holds in classroom teaching as well as in the law and other professions.

CHAPTER 8

Curriculum and Evaluation Issues

In this chapter the major problems and dilemmas related to curricular and evaluation decision making are presented to illustrate the moral complexity and at times uncertainty of professional life in the classroom. Beginning teachers face a common set of substantive problems and at times real dilemmas in their curricular and evaluation decision making. A second-year history teacher framed them as questions: "Should you teach material you don't appreciate the significance of (or believe that your students won't appreciate the significance of) just because it's in the curriculum?" "What reasons are just for passing or failing a student?" The first problem is, of course, part of a larger question that confronts all teachers: "What is worth knowing?" The second problem is also a corollary to a still larger question: "How does a teacher objectively and fairly judge competence and character?" In either case, the beginning teacher concludes, "The nature of these teaching dilemmas often prevents ultimate solutions."

DECIDING WHAT TO TEACH

What is worth knowing? This multifaceted question confronted this first-year suburban school teacher from almost the first day of teaching.

> One problem I have as a first-year teacher is going through some material I've never taught before and trying to keep up with the content: the facts and the dates of history. It's more than a question of being prepared, it's also turning around and having enough time to put it into a good lesson plan, something that the students are going to be involved with and that works well. So it's a challenge to try to "make history come alive." It's a challenge to bring that stuff to life; I always get the question: "Well, why do we have to study this stuff?" "What does it have to do with me?" Sometimes I have a problem answering that question. It's tough.

There are three dimensions to this teacher's problem that also resonate with the experiences of other beginning teachers: the difficulty of judging "What's worth knowing?" when you are learning the material for the first time yourself; the daily challenge of attempting to make the material meaningful and relevant to the students; and the deeper "So what?" question — in what way does this material serve my content and pedagogical goals? What are my criteria of selection — what if those standards of worth are violated?

Unfamiliar Subject Matter

There is a certain irony in discussing the "unpreparedness" of the liberally trained teacher to teach the subject matter. Yet, given the knowledge explosion of the modern world, almost all teachers in schools and universities face teaching courses in subjects in which they had no training as undergraduate or graduate students. This is particularly the case for social studies, English, and science teachers new to the field of secondary education. The results are predictable and perhaps unavoidable. An English teacher discusses her predicament during an interview conducted in February: "I still feel unprepared. Most teachers have stuff that they can fall back on, but I have to read a book that I've never read. I have to prepare totally something all new every day; everything is trial and error." A second-year science teacher in a boarding school echoes the English teacher's concerns. A biology major, she is teaching physics for the first time.

> The teaching crisis this year is not having a clue how to put physics lab equipment together. Every day I'm trying to figure out how to put the pieces together to have something valuable come out of the day; and it's very clear to me that I'm not doing as good a job in that course as I think I'm doing in my biology course.

However, one advantage these liberally educated teachers have going for them is the analytical skills they have acquired in college. Grossman, Wilson, and Shulman (1989) report on one first-year teacher interviewed in the Knowledge Growth in a Profession project: "[In teaching unfamiliar works], I'll be relying on just reading myself, picking out what I think are important themes, just because I'm experienced at doing that kind of thing in college" (p. 30). The beginning teachers in this study concur. But regardless of how well-equipped intellectually the beginning teacher is in meeting the challenge, "staying-one-chapter-ahead-of-the-student" teaching causes stress. "It's very tiring to me sometimes," reports an English teacher. "I get really burned out." However, until secondary schools change to accommodate to the needs of the beginning teacher by providing a teaching schedule that better fits the newcomer's "expertise," the task of learning the subject matter while teaching it for the first time will continue to plague many first-year teachers. The prospects for change in the immediate future are very unlikely.

Productive Learning

An equally pressing concern of the new teacher is the need and recurring demand on the part of students that the curriculum relate meaningfully to their lives and concerns. As a science teacher puts it, "You constantly hear, 'Why do we need science? I'm going to be a carpenter!'" The problem, of course, goes beyond adolescent egocentrism and shortsightedness. Without clear focus and time for reflection, a beginning teacher can also compound the problem. The English teacher recounts her first week of teaching.

> Because I was hired a week before classes and did not see a reading list until the day before I walked into a classroom, I had to do some things that I probably wouldn't have done. I did some reading skill exercises first off, which looking back I'd never do again. It was boring and stupid for them. They didn't get much out of it. It was just exercises to do so that the teacher could get a chance to catch up with the year and get ahead.

Such busy-work activities are not uncommon in schools. At times it is almost unavoidable given the beginning teacher's schedule and circumstances. But the issue cuts deeper. In observing the 19 teachers in their teaching, a substantive problem became apparent — in the words of the rural social studies teacher, "getting rid of the stuff that's nonproductive." A mathematics teacher in the same rural school put it in a more positive light: "There's so much more to do than there's time for; it's important to keep your horizon right close." Yet, when beginning teachers were asked, "How much of the class period involves productive learning? That is, students listening, discussing, or working independently or constructively in small groups," most of these beginners answered about half the class period. Here's a typical teacher response to the question.

> Interviewer: Since it's a 42-minute period, how much of that is productive learning?
> Beginner: Today — I would say probably 20 minutes.
> Interviewer: What percentage of the students were engaged in productive learning in the class?

Beginner: Probably 80%.

Interviewer: How long a time were the majority of your students attentive and with you during the lesson?

Beginner: I would say today probably 30 minutes; they were pretty with it today.

Interviewer: How well did the class go: Was it bad, fair, good, very good, excellent?

Beginner: Good.

Psychologizing Knowledge

There are, of course, many factors that may explain why beginners feel that about only half of the class period is spent in productive learning activities — limited student attention span, interruptions, lack of any interest on the part of students, and so forth. However, one cause is the pedagogical problem that Dewey (1974) identified in *The Child and the Curriculum* — "the material has not been translated into life-terms" (p. 352). Dewey's answer, of course, was the need for the teacher to "psychologize" the subject matter: "to transform the material, that is, to take it and to develop it within the range and scope of the child's life" (pp. 356–357). Feiman-Nemser and Buchmann (1985) also refer to this concept as "pedagogical thinking." It is "grounded in knowledge of self, children, and subject matter" (pp. 1–2). It also may be viewed as a problem in "learning the language of practice." As Yinger (1987) points out, the content of the subject matter is

> coded and understood in the language of theory and abstraction. The means for conveying this content must be coded in the language of concrete action and practice. Teachers must learn to juggle these disparate ways of thinking and acting, a task Brody has aptly referred to as uniting "the particularity of pupils with the universality of knowledge." (p. 67)

It appears, then, that beginning teachers need more help than they normally get in psychologizing the curriculum they are required to teach. Experienced teachers help as formal or informal mentors. But generally there is no systematic effort to walk a beginning teacher through the curriculum or to work with the novice on developing psychologized lesson plans that enhance student interest and lead to an increase in productive learning in the classroom. Until that happens much of the knowledge the liberally educated beginner possesses will remain, in Whitehead's (1929) term, "inert." Featherstone (1989) concurs: "Knowledge doesn't mean anything until it is remade in the present" (p. 32). That task in schools should be more collegial—involving beginner and veteran teachers working collaboratively to improve instruction.

Coverage

Determining what is worth knowing is, of course, the most difficult philosophical problem that both the beginning and the veteran teacher confront. When a first-year teacher was asked, "What do you worry most about as a teacher?" she replied: "Am I teaching the right things? Am I teaching them enough?" A first-year urban teacher puts it this way.

> There's so much information that I could give these kids—how much do I want to give to them and how much do I want to develop their thinking? So there have been times when I get all this information and I'm saying to myself, "How do I want to use it, what do I want to do with it?" And I get pulled from content to process.

A first-year social studies teacher focused on the problem in this way: "I worry about what if I'm not teaching kids something that they need to know? Is that going to hit them in a few years? Am I covering everything?" Thus the issue of coverage is of real concern to these beginners. Even a second-year teacher at an urban experimental school makes the same point but in reference to her school's philosophy.

> The first year the major dilemma was: "What am I supposed to teach?" I had an idea of how to teach it, but am I doing it correctly? That was a major conflict, which I don't have so much this year. But it's still a question in my mind. Now, it's more, "Am I teaching enough of what I'm supposed to teach?" It's hard for me to break away from the traditional curriculum. With the principle of "less is more," well, if "less is more" which "less" do I teach? How do I know that in the seventh and eighth grades—these division-one students when they go to division two in the ninth and tenth grades—will have the necessary skills to pass the exams that they have to take to enter high school?

The dilemma of coverage for this teacher and for the other beginning teachers relates to a personal concern that they are not teaching enough of the "right stuff" and that their "error of omission" will have unfortunate and unanticipated consequences for their students. Veteran teachers also

confront the coverage dilemma, but the problem may be defined differently. It may center more on an "error of commission." An experienced
suburban English teacher speaks about this form of the dilemma as it
relates to a department-wide final.

> It occurred during final examinations for my senior low-track stu-
> dents. These students have come a long way in their ability to sustain
> academic effort, to work cooperatively with their small learning com-
> munity, to read and to write better. Then they have to take an exami-
> nation that is irrelevant to what they have learned and irrelevant to
> their lives.
>
> Every one of them failed that part of the examination. They knew
> that they were failing as they were doing it, but they were so valiant in
> their attempt that I felt near tears. Not one complained. They simply
> worked item by item and did the best they could. I felt like screaming!
>
> It is too bad that sometimes we do not test what we teach. Back-
> ing up a bit, it is too bad that we do not think more carefully about
> what we would like the students to do before we make up examina-
> tions. I keep working on this problem, but progress is slow.

Thus the coverage dilemma cuts both ways: For inexperienced teachers
there is much self-questioning and feelings of inadequacy about what they
choose to teach and how they choose to teach it. For experienced teachers,
while these doubts never fully go away they may be compounded by department, school, or system-wide curriculum testing that may not make sense
in the context of the teachers' classrooms. In fact, the "tyranny of coverage"
may be deleterious to their students' learning and in conflict or opposition
to their goals as experienced, effective classroom teachers. There is, of
course, the other side of the argument. Standardized testing of this kind
may help increase or maintain teacher and school-wide accountability. It is
often argued that it helps insure that students are being taught the pre-
scribed curriculum that has been decided upon by the elected school committee and that reflects the community's norms, values, and educational
concerns. But unless teachers are convinced that certain "facts" are essential, this information will not be taught or taught well.

In the future, the problem of coverage and what is worth teaching
is likely to become an increasingly complex issue with deeper ideological
overtones for beginners as well as veteran teachers. The controversy over
Eurocentric versus Africentric curricular studies that is raging in many
ethnically diverse communities will perhaps make it even more difficult for
beginning teachers to decide what is worth knowing. Higher education
institutions—the liberal arts faculty as well as teacher educators—will need

to address the issue of multiculturalism and better prepare prospective teachers to reflect on and handle this politically charged issue in their classroom teaching.

THE TESTING OF COMPETENCE AND CHARACTER

Two grading controversies confront the beginning teacher as well as the more experienced teacher. The first of these difficult-to-handle problems is likely to arise at any time during the school year—that is, the problem of cheating by students. The second serious dilemma is likely to occur during the first or second marking period—making a tough decision on whether a student should pass or fail the quarter or the term. Two examples of each dilemma—those faced by the beginner and those confronted by the veteran—will help focus on the moral choices the teacher must often make in trying to be both objective and fair.

Cheating

A second-year suburban social studies teacher relates this incident of cheating.

> I was very set on integrity in my courses. I didn't want cheating and anything like that. But the problem was that I was giving these assignments that were conducive to cheating—for example, textbook-type answers to the textbook questions. In one of my classes I saw four kids who in that class had obviously just copied word for word off of each other's papers. This was in an honors class. So I called them all in, and they got very offended. I brought the assistant principal in, and he contacted the parents. It was a real crisis because it was, first of all, a confrontation with kids, which I wasn't used to; second was the fact that it dawned on me that maybe my policies had something to do with the misbehaving. If I had assigned a different type of assignment, it wouldn't have lent itself as closely to copying. I had to rethink what I was going to do.
>
> I stuck to my guns pretty much. I said, "This will be my policy, and if you choose to do the assignment over, you can get credit." I stuck to my guns, but I felt inside that I had to change things around. I even tried to patch things up with the kids.

Clearly this rookie mistake has been made by other first-year teachers who expect the moral behavior of college-bound students to be consistent with their own views of honesty and truth-telling. Yet, even experienced teachers sometimes face the problem of dealing with honor students who are up to "no good." The second example of cheating involves a veteran rural science teacher who left an examination for a substitute to administer to his college-bound students.

> I left a test with a substitute teacher. The kids were instructed by me, "This is a closed book exam. You have the question. You can organize your thoughts before class. When you write this test you may not use notes."
>
> The kids played with the substitute. They played, "Is this a test? We can use our notes." The sub was weak. The kids used their notes. I spent 15 to 20 hours reading exams thinking they had written them based on what was in their heads. Ugh!!!
>
> I got a tip. I was furious that the group would cooperate in this venture of cheating. The kids played dumb. "Everyone cheats." "You can't fail us all." "We weren't sure." "The substitute should have stopped us."
>
> I was ready to fail 'em all. Important lessons to be learned!!! The principal worried about the parents. Said the sub should have been strong. I am compromising my standards, but for peace I "regraded" each exam applying a standard that was tougher because I knew notes were used.

These incidents reveal the multilayered complexity of moral decision making. A "rookie mistake" caused a beginning teacher to re-examine her grading practices and to wrestle with and then refine her sense of fairness. A substitute's mistake and a principal's insistence forced a veteran teacher to compromise his standards and to readjust his criteria for grading. In both instances, it is very unclear what moral lessons students would have learned from the unfolding of events. Perhaps, the school remains more the "mirror" of society than an institution designed to transform and improve society.

The two examples of "the best and the brightest" students taking advantage of young or older teachers also demonstrate the "mutuality" of teaching. It is a term used by Erikson (1959) to indicate that the child has a reciprocal or "give and take" relationship with the adult that involves more than passively conforming to the rules or wishes of parents or other authority figures. For the beginning teacher's students, doing the teacher's busy work or boring assignments was met by both resistance and mischievousness. The absence of the authority figure represented by the experienced science teacher was perceived as an opportunity to test the limits in a playful but defiant way. In secondary education, the concept of mutuality must also be expanded to include parents and school administrators. These other sources of authority and power can serve to restrict options as well as place problems in the larger social or political context, which can be beneficial or detrimental depending on one's perspective and situation.

Under the pressure of circumstance and the political realities of the school culture, both the beginner and the veteran worked out pragmatic compromises to their quandaries. Were these *modi vivendi* acceptable? What impact would these compromises have on students and on the teachers' perceptions of themselves as professional educators? These questions, of course, cannot be answered definitively. But reflecting on them reveals the messiness as well as the moral and political nature of teaching. Philosophers often stress the importance of employing principled thought when engaging in practical moral reasoning—that is, "judging what is best to do in a particular teaching situation" (Strom, 1989, p. 270). Yet, as the experienced science teacher points out, compromise of one's principles may be necessary in conflictful teaching situations to keep the peace—even when one is the "victim of circumstances." The real world of business, the other professions, or the university is not far different. While it is critical not to commit the naturalistic fallacy, "What is, should be," it is also important to alert young teachers that it is not always possible to reconcile "moral dilemmas professionally and rationally" (Strom, 1989, p. 270). It is, however, just as important to emphasize that in most schools and in most crises the expedient course of action is the exception, not the rule.

Grading

The second pair of dilemmas involves teachers assigning final grades that will make a difference in the lives of their students. A first-year teacher who is also a football coach at a suburban high school must decide whether to pass or fail two of his players. The veteran teacher must decide whether to raise the passing grade of a "good kid" so that his parents will allow him to play baseball. Both dilemmas focus on the criteria for making a just and equitable evaluation of students' academic competence as well as character.

Here is the account of the first-year social studies teacher.

I've got two students in my U.S. history class—both of them play football and I have gotten to know them real well. I coach football here. Their grades were okay. They were both low seventies, and we had a big project due the last couple of weeks of the second term. They were supposed to complete three parts of the project: a timeline, a couple of biographies, and then analyze two primary sources. They weren't doing too well on them. They came real late to me and said that they really weren't doing too well. I really got upset because it had been a week and a half, and here they had two or three days to do it. "Why didn't you come to me before this?" "Well, you know, we thought we could get it done in the last few days." I'd been telling them all along it was going to take two weeks. They ended up doing half of the assignment. So I figured out their mathematical grades for the term and both ended up with right around 60–61, which does not pass here; 65 is passing.

And the dilemma that I faced is that U.S. history here is a semester course. If I gave them the 60, it would flunk them for the term, which would make them have to repeat the whole half year of U.S. history next year. And the choice I made, I'm not sure about. I said to them: "I really don't want you to repeat this whole course because I know you. You have been doing okay. You knew what was going on; I thought it would be a waste for you to repeat it next year." So I said, "I'm going to give you points to make it a 65, but next semester I'm going to take those points away from your final average." I basically told them, "I'm giving you a break. I hope this is an incentive to get your butts going in the classroom." It's worked so far; they've been more than conscientious, so far. But it was really a dilemma of compromising. I felt like I kind of compromised principle by giving points away when I didn't with other students. But at the same time I felt that it was worth it because of the motivation and the idea of having them repeat a whole half year when they could be taking something else. I really fought with it for a couple of days, and that was the decision I reached. I'm still not sure if it's a right or a wrong one.

Did this young teacher make the right decision? Would an experienced teacher have made a similar choice? Interestingly, a similar dilemma about a student who wants to play baseball is described in a recent book by a rural Vermont teacher (Keizer, 1988). The student receives a C from the teacher. His mother has told him, "Anything less than a B, and you don't play baseball" (p. 63). After some negotiation with the teacher, the student is able to raise his mark to a C+. The teacher then goes to the parents' home to support the son's plea to be allowed to play ball even though his grade is not sufficient. The teacher argues the son's case, but the mother's reply is that her son "is capable of an A," which the teacher also believes. The teacher then adds he is willing to give the student a "point loan." The teacher states that the student can "take what he needed to make a mark of B, and pay up at the end of the next marking period." The teacher has done this several times before, and he says, "I would have no qualms doing so for someone like [your son]. [The boy] is an honest young man and he's never been a complainer" (p. 64). The student's father now responds:

> [My son] is an honest young man, that's a fact. He works hard, at least on the farm. His mother says he could work harder at school, and she is probably right. But it is a hard thing to say to a boy, you cannot play baseball. It is hard on us, and it is hard on him. I think maybe we are too hard — then I think we are too easy. There is no way to know. (pp. 64–65)

As might be predicted, the high school student is allowed to play baseball that season.

While the two dilemmas are similar in terms of the three athletes not making the grade when all were fully capable of performing at that level or higher, there are differences, too. The punishment for the football players would be repeating a course that they could handle intellectually and forgoing another elective in their senior year; for the baseball player, it would mean not participating in a sport he loves. I think most of us would feel better about giving the baseball player the break; at least he was not "goofing off" and trying to take advantage of the player–coach relationship. But he was also not fulfilling his academic potential and possibly precluding life options that his mother desperately wanted open to him. With this perspective in mind, it is not at all clear that the seven-year veteran teacher was really doing the baseball player a favor. Perhaps the baseball player rather than the football players needs to be "taught the hard lesson." Nonetheless, each dilemma is a hard choice that carries costs for the teacher as well as the student, no matter what path is taken. Moral decision making of this kind not only tests but reveals the character of the teacher as well as the other participants in the dilemma. Robert Coles (1986) is fond of quoting Walker Percy's insightful observation: "You can get all A's and still flunk life" (p. 29). Both the beginning teacher and the experienced teacher passed the test of character and competence with regard to how they handled their grading quandaries. However, there would probably be an argument over what passing marks they should receive.

When the beginning teacher's dilemma was presented in a seminar to a group of teacher educators, education foundations faculty, and department administration staff, the responses varied markedly. Some teacher educators said the equivalent of, "No way, the students should have flunked." Others agreed with the new teacher's basic decision; still others would have given the two students an incomplete. There are, of course, still other possible alternatives. This problem reveals the full range of moral ambiguities and personal and social interactions that have significance both in and out of the classroom.

CHAPTER 9

Professional Concerns
and Support

In this chapter the focus is on the beginning teachers' professional concerns and their commitment to their careers as teachers. What is their workload? Is job stress a serious problem? How satisfied and committed to a career in teaching are these young professionals? What attracts and what might hold them in teaching? Finally, what is the cycle of the academic year like for them? Are there patterns of events that affect them that are similar to or different from those that veteran teachers experience?

TIME DEMANDS

Workload

Both beginning teachers and experienced teachers were asked to calculate their weekly workloads. Shown in Table 9.1 are average workloads of 19 beginning teachers[1] and 25 veteran teachers who participated in the spring survey. Again, it is important to note the limitations of self-reporting. The statistics may or may not reflect the actual work week of this sample of beginning and veteran teachers. The findings do, however, indicate that these teachers judge that they put in long hours in their multi-faceted professional role.

Given the sample of inexperienced and experienced high-achieving teachers, the results are not too surprising. First, as might have been anticipated, the total hours per week at school and at home are higher than in other recent survey findings. In Goodlad's (1984) study of 1,350 elementary, junior high, and high school teachers, he indicates a "minimum of

---

1. The workloads of two independent boarding school teachers were not included because their full-time schedule of over 90 hours a week would skew the results, making it appear that beginning teachers on average work a much longer work week than their more experienced colleagues.

Table 9.1. Teachers' Weekly Workload

Where Time Spent	Hours	
	Beginners	Veterans
In school	46	42
At home	11	13
Total	57	55

37-1/2 hours of work per week, a modal range of 40 to 45, and a high of just over 50" (p. 170). An earlier National Education Association survey (1967) reported a mean of just over 47 hours weekly for teachers. Second, there was no appreciable difference between the work week of the novice and the veteran teacher. Each puts in a "long" week both in school and at home. However, since many of these newcomers hold the belief that "things will get better" for them after a few years of teaching, it is important that they realize that staying "on top of teaching" may require less mental strain but just as many hours of hard work as they are now putting into the job.

Job Stress

Since the average workload is substantial, how stressful is the job for the 21 beginning and 25 veteran teachers who participated in the spring survey? The data suggest that the majority of younger (71%) and older (60%) teachers feel teaching is mildly to moderately stressful but that an appreciable number of both groups (beginners, 28%; veterans, 36%) find teaching very stressful. The heavy workload, of course, contributes principally to the job stress of the new teachers. The role of stress in the work lives of new and veteran teachers is described in the four responses that follow.

Second-Year Teacher
There are so many kids I need to pull aside and do coaching kind of stuff—working more one-on-one, calling home. I just don't have the wherewithal. I'm just too exhausted. Obviously the biggest problem is the workload. I'm still working 60 hours a week and I'm just overwhelmed by that.

Another Second-Year Teacher
My major problem this year is that I am really fatigued—the lack of energy to do all the work that is required; no energy to really think of brand-new ways to approach things.

First-Year Teacher

> I'm here by 7:00 a.m. and with coaching I usually don't leave until 7:00 or 8:00 p.m. at night. That leaves me a couple of hours a night to prepare. Monday through Friday, I literally do nothing but teach and coach and do lesson plans.

Experienced Science Teacher

> Ugh. No wonder I am burned out!!! I really do prepare my own activities and lessons, and require essay answers on tests and many reports. How can you learn to think without writing?

The multiple role demands of "good teaching" make the professional life of the new teacher and the veteran teacher with high standards taxing and at times exhausting. Other studies, too, have identified the principal cause of anxiety of teachers as a "shortage of time" (Coates & Thorensen, 1976). Thus the lack of spare time seems to be an occupational hazard that will not necessarily go away with time. Professionals in other occupations face the same dilemma of trying to do all that is needed and still have time for family and some relaxation during the work week. However, these people are often rewarded with better salaries and higher professional prestige. A second-year teacher makes that telling point when discussing the times when she is most stressed out: "I am up at 5:30 a.m. straight 'til bedtime for a week. The kids are unmotivated and hyper; I have tests to grade, homework to correct, research and lesson planning to pull together, and materials to create; and an acquaintance tells me teachers have it easy." The real issue, of course, for young teachers—and the teaching profession in general—is how to learn to cope better with job stress while maintaining their pride and commitment to good teaching.

PROFESSIONAL COMMITMENT

Given the heavy workload, low wages, and low status, how committed to teaching are these beginning teachers? This is a particularly important question since over 30% of beginning teachers leave the profession by the end of the fifth year. Most often, those who decide to pursue other career paths are the "most academically talented individuals" who enter the field (Rosenholtz, 1987, p. 15).

Indications of Satisfaction

Besides the number of hours teachers commit to the job, three other ways to gauge the beginners' commitment to their careers are by ascertain-

Table 9.2. Teacher Satisfaction with Occupation:
All Beginning and Veteran Teachers

	Percentage	
Degree of Satisfaction	Beginners	Veterans
Extremely satisfied	24	32
Very satisfied	45	32
More satisfied than not	18	24
Equally satisfied/dissatisfied	8	12
Dissatisfied	5	0

ing from them the degree of satisfaction they get from teaching, their readiness to repeat their occupational decision, and their assessment of their career prospects five years down the line. The beginning and the experienced teachers were asked questions drawn from Lortie's (1975) study and an earlier National Education Association (1967) survey of over 1,000 teachers. All 38 beginning teachers responded to these questions in the fall. Twenty-one beginners also answered them again in the spring. These 21 teachers' fall and spring responses are included in the following tables, to chart whether any significant change occurred in their attitude and commitment toward teaching as a career. Tables 9.2 and 9.3 illustrate what the beginners and veterans revealed about their present level of satisfaction with, and their present and future commitment to, the teaching profession.

It appears that beginning teachers and veteran teachers are generally "more" than satisfied with their jobs and, in fact, for a number of the beginning teachers in the sample of 21, job satisfaction seems to have increased over the course of the academic year. (For example, in Table 9.3 beginners selecting very satisfied or extremely satisfied with their job increased from 67% to 86% over the course of the school year.) Lagana (1970) hypothesizes that there may be a "curve of disenchantment" at work

Table 9.3. Teacher Satisfaction with Occupation:
Fall and Spring Survey Ratings (21 Beginning Teachers)

	Percentage	
Degree of Satisfaction	Fall rating	Spring rating
Extremely satisfied	24	19
Very satisfied	43	67
More satisfied than not	24	5
Equally satisfied/dissatisfied	9	5
Dissatisfied	0	4

Table 9.4. Teachers' Willingness to Choose to Teach Again:
All Beginning and Veteran Teachers and 1967 NEA Study

Degree of Willingness	Percentage		
	Beginners	Veterans	NEA study
Certainly would	46	40	45
Probably would	38	20	26
Chances about even	10	20	16
Probably would not	3	20	10
Certainly would not	3	0	3

during the beginning teachers' first four months of teaching. Their attitudes toward their students during this time are less positive than those of prospective teachers just entering formal training. During the second half of the academic year, the beginning teachers' attitudes level out and begin a slight rise. To some degree, this phenomenon may be at work with some of the beginning teachers in this study and may help explain the increase in their job satisfaction ratings. In any case, it is an encouraging indication that beginning teachers do not become disillusioned about teaching but rather may even draw increased satisfaction from their work with adolescents.

Included in the National Education Association survey (1967) was a question about readiness to repeat one's occupational decision. As Table 9.4 indicates, the results of the "secondary teachers' willingness to teach again" item were similar to the finding in this study for beginning teachers but not necessarily for veteran teachers. As Table 9.5 also indicates, the beginning teachers' vocational decision seems fairly firm at this point in their careers, but many of the veteran teachers are equivocal about or

Table 9.5. Teachers' Willingness to Choose to Teach Again:
Fall and Spring Survey Ratings (21 Beginning Teachers)

Degree of Willingness	Percentage	
	Fall rating	Spring rating
Certainly would	43	43
Probably would	43	38
Chances about even	14	14
Probably would not	0	5
Certainly would not	0	0

seem to regret their lifework decision. While it is unclear why many of the experienced teachers are less sure about their vocational decision, a number of female veteran teachers in the cooperating teacher sample were highly competent teachers who may not have perceived other options at the time they made their commitment to teaching as a career. They and some of their male counterparts may also have entered teaching during the Kennedy era when public service was more valued and rewarded than it was in the 1970s and early 1980s. Now, as in the 1960s, the beginning teachers are entering the profession at a time of educational reform and the promise of better salaries and working conditions. Many of these educators are interested in devoting their working lives to public service careers. Like the veteran teachers, it is probable that their long-term professional commitment will be affected by whether the promises of educational reform and renewal are kept by our national and state leaders, and carried out by the elected officials and parents in their school district.

What, then, do the beginning teachers and their veteran colleagues envision as their career prospects? In the fall semester of their first year of teaching, 65% of the beginners indicated that they would still be in teaching in five years. Sixteen percent believed they would be working in another profession, and 8% felt they would be going to a graduate or professional school. Another 11% were unclear about their career plans in the next five years. Over 70% of the veteran teachers indicated they would still be in teaching in five years. The others contemplated that they would be in graduate school (12%) or be retired from teaching (16%) by then. In the spring, of the 21 teachers reporting, 67% as compared with 62% of the same subgroup when responding in the fall survey indicated they expected to be teaching in five years.

The "one-third rule" seems to hold for both young and older teachers. Just as other studies have shown, about one-third of the new teachers may drop out of teaching by the fifth year. Some of these young teachers will become college professors or school administrators, and will thus remain in education. Others, it appears, think of teaching as an "interim engagement" and anticipate leaving teaching for law or business school — much as many bright and articulate teachers in the late 1960s did. Still others have made only a provisional commitment to teaching at this point — they may continue or they may move on. Lortie's (1975) findings seem to hold today as well. In teaching there is a certain "tentativeness of future commitment" (p. 86). Given teaching's uncertain role and status in society, the situation is unlikely to change in the near future. It is clear though that more effort must be put into the retention as well as the training of these young professionals if the statistics are to turn significantly upward.

Attracting and Retaining Liberally Educated Teachers

The four beginners featured in Part I—Wendy, Maria, James, and Elizabeth—were asked to reflect on how liberally educated individuals from select colleges and universities can be attracted to and retained in public school teaching. Their views are similar to those of other beginners in larger samples of teachers who responded to national surveys in the late 1960s and 1970s. The four beginning teachers talk about both internal and external factors, and, like teachers in the earlier national surveys, they clearly come down on the side of the psychic rewards that were critical to their decisions to teach (Lortie, 1975). Maria Fernandez believes

> You have to be committed. You have to have it coming from within yourself. The commitment that you want to be an influence on students. You can't do anything in particular that is external unless you count seeing the students succeeding. It's an intrinsic thing for me.

Elizabeth Alberto speaks in a similar vein.

> It's hard to explain what attracts people to teaching. It certainly isn't the money, the job security, or respect as a professional, because they don't exist—especially for a beginning teacher. There were times when my job for the next year was not certain, when I wondered why I wanted to teach. The truth is that I love working with the students, and no other job could give me the kind of emotional reward teaching can. Of course, increasing the salary and the job security wouldn't hurt either!

Wendy Light, too, agrees that it is the "students" but also the "ability to keep learning" that attracted her and sustains her in teaching. However, she says:

> I hate to say it but money and respect also are important. Especially people who graduate from a school like mine—it's costly. Many don't want to graduate from a school like that and just be a teacher. But then you have to question the type of people who are just going after the money and prestige. We want people who are really committed to young people and who want to continue their own education. That's what it's all about.

Finally, in responding from his perspective, James Crawford-Williams concludes that more people like him would be attracted to teaching if there was a reasonable workload in a more humane school environment, less bureaucratic red tape in the teacher licensing process, and, of course, greater individual freedom and power for the teacher in the workplace. He elaborates:

> The institutional norms have to be such that people can survive in the institution itself. That means the student load as well as the course load have to be good. You have to have the type of freedom for people to approach a subject in their own way.
>
> We also have to find a way of downplaying but not ignoring the types of standards we have set up for teachers to meet before they can go into the classroom. The teacher training programs are really trying to make a teacher a certain way, and I don't think that lends itself to real learning. So we have to find a way to get school districts not to stress certification so much, not be primarily concerned with where people learn to teach, just give people the opportunity—see what they can do.

In his 1975 publication, *Schoolteacher*, Lortie lists five major attractors to teaching.

1. Interpersonal—desire to work with young people
2. Service—performing a mission of special moral worth
3. Continuation—liking school and wanting to continue learning
4. Material benefits
5. Time compatibility—flexible work schedules

As is apparent, the four newcomers, like most other teachers in national surveys, rank working with students as the primary reason for entering the profession. Implicit in their comments and made more explicit in each of their case studies is their other principal reason for teaching. They view teaching as a vocation with a special mission in our society, a calling, in fact, possibly requiring material and psychological sacrifice. Other teachers in the national surveys also rank the service theme as a close second in importance to their involvement with the young. Of tertiary concern are, of course, increased material benefits. Finally, only James Crawford-Williams explicitly states as a substantive reason for undertaking his calling the desire to change the system radically.

The implications are clear. To attract and keep more people like Maria, James, Elizabeth, and Wendy in teaching fundamentally requires the encouragement and recognition by our society that teaching is a vital and uplifting profession. While making clear that a career in teaching necessitates commitment, service, and some financial sacrifice, our national leaders must work to improve the material benefits and working conditions of teachers as a whole. These liberally educated teachers are not asking for miracles. They want and deserve greater respect and appreciation, and the enabling conditions in the schools that permit them to do their jobs well. They need increased salaries as well. Perhaps substantive school reform is needed, as James Crawford-Williams argues so eloquently. He is, of course, supported by a growing chorus of educators, business leaders, and politicians. Yet, I suspect most of the beginners in this study and nationwide would settle for a gradual but steady improvement in the conditions of teaching. One such practical school-based reform — improved mentorship — is the focus of Chapter 10.

CYCLE OF TEACHING

As a rite of passage, the first year of teaching is full of critical events and turning points. The cycle of teaching for beginning teachers is revealed through a series of chart illustrations that depict these memorable moments. Clearly, during the initial year on the job, the teacher is challenged and tested by students and by the other "publics," including at times school administrators, other teachers, and parents. When does the testing of the newcomer to the profession begin? When is the most difficult time of teaching? When is the best time? When does the first-year teacher begin to feel "on top of the job"? There are also events that happen to almost all teachers as the academic year unfolds, such as communicating with parents about their child or talking to a school administrator about a student who has a behavioral or academic problem. There are better times as well: receiving the first compliment or experiencing the first teaching triumph of the year. In the spring questionnaire both beginners and veterans were asked to indicate when these various events may have happened to them during the academic year. Some interesting patterns are suggested by their responses. But as important as some of the emerging group configurations are the unique, diverse, and unexpected patterns of classroom life of the individual beginning or veteran teachers. For example, the time when a teacher really got to know most of his or her students may have happened in the early, middle, or late part of the academic year. In certain cases, it may not have happened at all to first-year or veteran teachers. The cycle of teaching is set up to depict the "ups and downs" of teaching, "the best of times and worst of times," the times of greatest challenge to the teacher's classroom authority and control, and the time of the teacher's greatest (and growing) sense of competence and effectiveness in the classroom.

Responses of 20 of the beginning teachers and the 25 veterans were tabulated. The figures in this chapter and in the Appendix indicate in percentage by month how each group viewed each cyclical event. Certain of the data stand out for further analysis. Figure 9.1 suggests that many beginners feel that the first four months of teaching were most difficult, with December being a particularly hard time for 40% of them, rather than October as many professional educators would have predicted. Many of the veterans who reported having difficulty selected the second half of the academic year, with May and June combined being the toughest months for 44% of those teachers. For the veterans, the last two months of the school year may often be most difficult because of end of the year paper work, the need to cover so much material in too short a time, and the general restiveness of the students, who are looking forward to summer vacation or graduation. And, of course, there is just plain fatigue of an older faculty.

Why is December the most problematic time for some new teachers? It probably involves the following combination of factors: First, the teachers are often struggling under an avalanche of paper work, have exhausted their repertoire of innovative or creative teaching strategies, and contemplate spending much of their vacation correcting papers and getting out from under. Second, students often become itchy and slack off in their work just before the holidays. Third, the beginner—perhaps just out of college or graduate school—is adjusting to a new work cycle, one without so much time off after semester finals. As one beginner put it, "There were too many commitments at Christmas time—both school-related and personal."

Figure 9.1. Most Difficult Time of Teaching

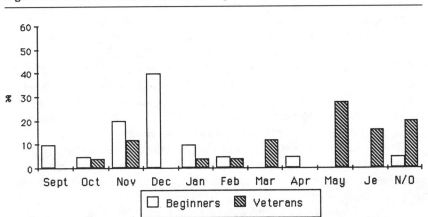

Figure 9.2. Time Most Needed Help/Support

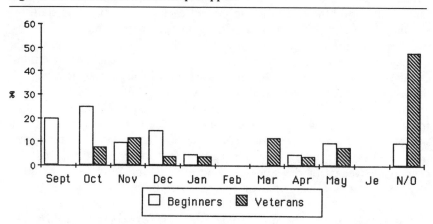

The data from questions that dealt with classroom discipline and control indicate another principal reason why the beginning months of teaching are considered problematic by many beginners. It appears that classroom management is likely to be a problem from the start of the school year for the beginning teacher, with the months of September and October being the time of greatest testing and challenging. For example, gaining effective classroom discipline is the most serious problem during these two months for 50% of the teachers. A beginning teacher is likely to give a detention or talk to an administrator about a discipline problem in the first 60 days of teaching. This pattern is predictable. Yet, through this initial period of testing of the beginner's authority and mettle, school administrators and older faculty traditionally seem to adopt a more reactive than proactive stance — often letting the teachers deal with problems as best they can and intervening only when necessary. The comments of this urban teacher reflect this usual state of affairs. She says, "I had a class first quarter full of kids who had decided before they arrived that they didn't like school, etc. They fed on each other, and I had to really deal with discipline problems as I never had during student teaching." The young teacher had to work things out on her own. As she says, "I did not receive much helpful mentoring." Perhaps that "sink or swim" practice needs to be re-examined.

Figure 9.2 indicates that the first four months of the academic year are also the time that many of the teachers (70%) could use a "helping hand." While several of the beginners indicate that late spring may be when they need more help, it appears that most beginners need special nurturing during the first semester. It is likely to be the "time of troubles" for them in

both their classrooms and their personal lives. What kind of help did some
of these teachers feel they needed? A suburban first-year teacher says that
by the end of the third month, "I was tired and felt like the only thing I did
in life was teaching/schoolwork. I got emotional support from my colleagues and my department chair." During the same month, another
teacher, who taught in a rural school, also needed emotional support. He
states, "One of my classes was really getting to me, and I sought out two
teachers who'd had that class last year. I felt better when I learned they'd
had the same problems as I had." A suburban beginning teacher had a
rough time with classroom discipline in October. She describes her plight
this way: "In my second month of teaching, classroom management was
impossible. My curricular choices were not well-informed. I talked to the
principal for tips on discipline." Finally, a beginning teacher at an independent school felt "stressed out" at the end of the academic year. He discusses
his problem in these terms: "You realize you are behind where you should
be to complete the planned objectives for the year. You coach three hours
a day, six days a week. And seniors in your dorm are all out of control
anticipating graduation. Too much pressure, too little time."

Regardless of the time of year, it is important that the beginner know
that not only is help available, but that it is expected that the newcomer
will need extra support from time to time. It should, therefore, become the
norm, not the exception, that a beginner will seek and be given help.

Turning to the more positive aspects of their first-year odyssey, as
Figure 9.3 indicates, the best months of teaching for the majority of beginners were the second half of the academic year—about the time it began to

Figure 9.3. Best Month of Teaching

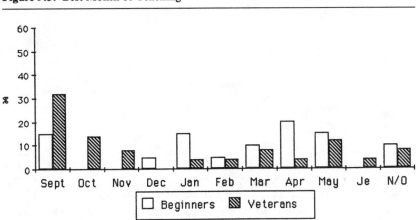

go downhill for many veteran teachers. In a similar vein, beginners were asked when they felt on top of teaching. It seems that there is no discernible pattern when a beginning teacher is likely to feel "in charge and on top of things." It may happen in October or in June, or in the case of several of the teachers, not at all. This more gradual or attenuated process of the beginning teachers contrasts strikingly with the veteran teachers, the majority of whom feel "on top of it" by the end of the second month of the school year. Yet, even some of them report that they did not really get "on top of it" by the end of the second month of the school year. And, some of them even report that they did not really get "on top of it" during any month of the teaching year. Getting on top of teaching may, of course, mean different things to different teachers. One suburban teacher remarked, "It is difficult to describe—things just seem to click." Nevertheless, it might do well for all of us to spell out more precisely what it means. It might be even better on occasion to ask the new teachers what it means to them. With a clearer picture of how they feel about their teaching, some new course of action might be suggested to them at different times during the academic year.

Figure 9.4 reveals when the beginning teacher "really felt like a real teacher." Sixty-five percent of them reported they had achieved this status by the end of December, almost all of them by May. Yet, three beginners reported still not feeling they were yet full-fledged teachers. Their reasons were understandable. A second-year teacher sums it up: "In teaching, it's a hard job to be a beginner. I'm still a beginner. Two years down the line and I still have so much to learn. I'm so much better than before—but jeez."

Figure 9.4. Beginners—Time Felt Were "Real" Teacher

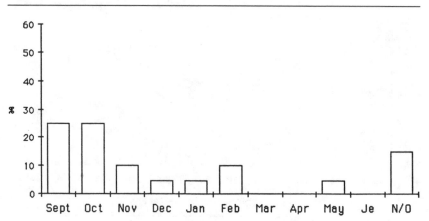

Yet, most beginners had reason to be upbeat about their prospects, as indicated by the responses to the question: When did you receive your first compliment? By the end of November, 75% of them reported that students had paid them a compliment such as "You're cool" or "This is really fun. I really like this project." Other compliments included "A boy left a note on my car to have a nice weekend"; "She's not really a 'teacher,' she just knows more than us"; and "This is only your first year? You're really good."

Given the small sample, these findings are preliminary regarding the cycle of teaching. While they have limited predictive value, they raise some tentative hypotheses that need to be explored further in other research studies. Should some of these findings be confirmed—for example, about when a beginning teacher is likely to have discipline problems or need the most help—this information could prove valuable to the teachers, to their department chairs, and to other school administrators in devising more effective orientation and follow-up programs.

CHAPTER 10

Mentorship

The mentorship of beginning teachers who participated in the study was a particular focus of inquiry for two major reasons: first, to determine to what degree "learning to teach" is a self-socialization process and to what degree it is a collaborative effort on the part of the beginner and various colleagues and supervisors; and second, to assess how mentorship is regarded as an educational reform by beginning and veteran teachers in the study and by the education profession as a whole.

SELF-SOCIALIZATION OF BEGINNING TEACHERS

In 1966, Lortie compared the beginning teacher's entry year of teaching to Robinson Crusoe's struggle for survival.

> As for Defoe's hero, the beginning teacher may find that prior excellence supplied him with some alternatives for action, but his crucial learning comes from his personal errors; he fits together solutions and specific problems into some kind of whole and at times finds leeway for the expression of personal tastes. Working largely alone, he cannot make the specifics of his working knowledge base explicit, nor need he, as his victories are private. (p. 59)

In Lortie's view learning to teach is, in reality, a process of self-socialization, involving independent trial-and-error learning. Because of this emphasis on "learning while doing," the lack of a "common technical culture," and the professional isolation of the newcomer from his or her colleagues, most teachers come to adopt a utilitarian view: If it works, use it (pp. 60–61). This is a variation of what Rousseau (1762/1979) terms in *Emile* the "law of utility." "What is that good for? This is now the sacred word, the decisive word . . . in all actions of our life" (p. 179). Complementing this pragmatic view of teaching is the school-wide, hands-off ethic; let the new teacher "sink or swim." This ethic allows for a large degree of teacher autonomy and self-expression in the classroom, but it also leads to errors of judgment and to failure. As a second-year teacher remarked, "You are going to make a ton of mistakes your first year, and you should not let that get to you. You should not judge your teaching abilities by your first year in teaching. Because if everyone did that, we would have no teachers left."

How accurate a portrait does Lortie paint of "learning to teach"? Does the pattern still hold today? From this study of beginning teachers, the answer is a qualified "yes and no." On most levels, Lortie's (1966, 1975) description of beginning teaching still holds up. The formative learning experience is still obtained on the job, without much systematic and substantive help from colleagues and supervisors. Teachers remain largely autonomous in the classroom and often are left to "wing it." Given the dynamics of classroom life, they plan the best they can, improvise when necessary, make good and bad decisions, and manage to "survive with dignity" through hard work and their considerable "brain power." Beginners face most major decisions on their own. Through such an odyssey, a self-constructed professional identity is often successfully formed. In fact, most of those polled in the spring considered the academic year a success. While the criteria of success, of course, vary, most of the beginners had similar experiences to those of the four new teachers depicted in the case studies; they held their own and then some. Their criteria were based on their initial expectations of first-year teaching, as compared with their veteran colleagues who had their previous years of experience upon which to judge their own effectiveness. As Table 10.1 indicates, three-quarters of the 21 beginning teachers rated their academic year either "above average" or "a great success." Their ratings are comparable to the experienced teachers'. As might be anticipated, the only appreciable difference in the two sets of ratings is that more veterans (32%) than beginners (15%) considered their year "a great success."

Table 10.1. Rating the Year's Teaching Success

| Degree of Success | Percentage | |
	Beginners	Veterans
Great	15	32
Above average	60	36
Average	25	24
Below average	0	8

While most of the beginning teachers learned to teach mainly on their own, a number of the novices did receive some form of mentoring during their first year of teaching, as do many other teachers across the nation.

FUNCTION OF MENTORS

As Daniel Levinson (1978) notes in *The Seasons of a Man's Life*, "The mentor relationship is one of the most complex, and developmentally important, a man can have in early adulthood" (p. 97). Levinson believes this is equally true for women in the workplace (p. 98). Besides at times acting as a teacher in helping develop a person's intellectual skills, Levinson asserts the mentor may also serve as a sponsor, host, and guide, "welcoming the initiate into a new occupational and social world and acquainting him with its values, customs, resources and cast of characters" (p. 98). The mentor also serves as an exemplar that the neophyte may admire and seek to emulate. The mentor, of course, provides "counsel and moral support in times of stress" (p. 98). In Hennig and Jardim's 1977 study of women in business, the mentors, who were at that time almost all males in the business world, also played a similar role for young women executives. "To each woman," they report, "[her mentor] was her supporter, her encourager, her teacher and her strength in the company. He admired her competence and her will to succeed" (p. 129).

While all these roles of the mentor are important, Levinson (1978) contends that the mentor's most important function, and developmentally the most crucial one, is to

> support and facilitate the realization of the Dream. . . . He fosters the young adult's development by believing in him, sharing the youthful Dream and giving it his blessing, helping to define the newly emerging self in its newly discovered world, and creating a space in which the young man can work on a reasonably satisfactory life structure that contains the Dream. (pp. 98–99)

Gilligan's (1982) work on women's development suggests that the mentoring process and the Dream may be somewhat different for women. Like the development of personal identity, most women's professional identity is formed and "defined in the context of relationships and judged by the standard of responsibility and care" (p. 160). Mentoring for many women then implies the fulfillment of their Dream in relation to others' dreams, and in ways that nurture their personal development as well as that of significant others. Individualization—carving out the space—is often less important than building relationships based on the "adult ethic of taking care" (p. 164). Therefore, the relationship between the mentor and the protégé becomes an end in itself for many women.

MENTORING PROGRAMS

Because of its recognized importance developmentally in other professions and in the business community as well, mentorship of beginning teachers began as an educational reform in the early 1980s and has spread rapidly throughout our nation's schools. Many researchers and practitioners in schools assert that the first year is the critical year, for it "often determines whether a person will stay in teaching and what type of teacher the person will become" (Shulman & Colbert, 1988, p. 1). More than 28 states, including California, Connecticut, Massachusetts, Florida, and Oklahoma, have mandated some form of mentorship program for beginning teachers. The California Mentor Teacher Program was one of the earliest large-scale, state-mandated programs to be established in the early 1980s. The California Board of Education requires that all first-year teachers be mentored. Mentors are paid $4,000 stipends and given released days to work with their protégés. Their primary role is to guide and assist new teachers, but it is up to each school district to determine what kind of program will be put in place (California State Department of Education, 1983). Consequently, attempting to evaluate the state-wide impact of California's program is difficult. As Laura Wagner (1985), administrator of the California Mentor Program, states:

> How can useful evaluation be conducted when program goals are intangible and hard to operationalize, when "the program" is different at every site at which it operates, when evaluation has not been mandated from the program's inception, when required documentation is absolutely minimal. (p. 1)

Implementation of the mentorship program also varies greatly in other states. For instance, while a plan has been on the books for some years, the Commonwealth of Massachusetts has yet to start its program calling for a first-year internship in which the beginner is to be guided and supported by a paid, trained mentor. The lack of clear goals and funds to implement the educational reform results in unevenness in the quality of teacher mentor programs. Arthur Wise (cited in Kolbert, 1987) claims that "most people who are creating internship programs are not serious about it. People are trying to run these programs on the cheap" (p. 24). As Kolbert (1987) states:

> There is no one way to be a mentor, and programs vary widely from state
> to state and school to school. . . . In some cases, mentors work only with
> one intern, in others several. In some cases they are supposed to help
> interns master specific skills, in others their mandate is more diffuse. (pp.
> 22–24)

For a mentor program to be effective, Wise argues that "mentor teachers
must be freed from at least 10 percent of their teaching loads" (p. 24). Few
mentor programs provide such released time for experienced teachers. In
the California Mentor Program mentor teachers are given only 10 days a
year to perform their various responsibilities. Almost all the "grass-roots"
mentorship programs provide no released time at all. Experienced teachers
are expected to volunteer the extra time and put in the extra effort as part
of their professional obligations as teachers.

   There are, however, two large-scale mentorship programs that are
well-designed, with clear goals and adequate funding to sustain the innovation. These are the Albuquerque Public Schools/University of New Mexico Graduate Intern/Teacher Induction Program and the Toledo Public
Schools/Toledo Federation of Teachers Toledo Internship Program. In
each program mentors are released full-time from the classroom to perform
their mentoring responsibilities with beginning teachers. The Albuquerque
program stresses teacher reflection and the uniting of theory and practice
in the classroom and seminar. The Toledo program emphasizes the "nuts
and bolts" approach to teaching, with a strong emphasis on classroom
discipline in the urban school.

Albuquerque Program

   According to Stoddart and Feiman-Nemser (1988), the Albuquerque
Public Schools/University of New Mexico Graduate Intern/Teacher Induction Program began in 1984 in response to a New Mexico State Board of
Education mandate that school districts provide support to first-year teachers. Currently, the graduate program involves 28 beginning teachers who
serve as interns in the city schools while earning a master's degree from the
university. They participate in coursework during the summer before and
after the school year. They also take concurrent courses during the school
year. The public schools release 17 veteran teachers to work with the University of New Mexico School of Education. Nine of the teachers work in
the undergraduate methods courses at the university. The other eight teachers are designated as clinical-support teachers who help the graduate interns
and other first-year teachers in the school system. To be selected, the experi-

enced teachers must have taught at least five years and have on file letters of support indicating they are superior teachers who can work well with adults. Support teachers normally work with between 15 and 18 new teachers, including three or four graduate interns. They are given a week-long orientation to their new positions and are expected to serve for two years in their roles.

They work closely with beginning teachers in the novices' classrooms and attend a seminar each week on teaching/learning. At these seminars, they discuss research on teacher development and the induction process and have an opportunity to share experiences and solve problems. Twice a month the clinical-support teachers lead seminars with the beginning teachers with whom they work.

The clinical-support teachers provide help and advice to new teachers in seven areas: system information, resources/materials, instruction, emotional issues, classroom management, classroom environment, demonstration teaching. They do not serve as evaluators. That function is performed solely by school administrators. The emphasis of the program is on "reflective, analytical teaching with a child-centered focus" that stresses active learning in the elementary school classroom (Stoddart & Feiman-Nemser, 1988, p. 86). In helping beginning teachers employ innovative practices in the regular classroom, the clinical-support teachers are key. They help "link theory and practice, offering ideas, materials and support" (p. 87). They also are involved in team teaching with the beginners in the classroom and serve as the novice teachers' advocates.

Because interns are paid half the salary of a regular first-year teacher by the university, the funds freed up for the school system by not hiring 28 new teachers pay for the release of the mentor teachers. It results in a "no additional cost" exchange and fosters the continuation of the school-university collaboration. According to Sandra Odell, director of the graduate intern program, the reason the program works so well is the collegial and purposeful nature of the relationship. She states:

> Although the support teachers have considerable experience from which to draw, they still are perceived as colleagues. Often they will teach side by side in a classroom with a beginning teacher. The support teachers say this offers an opportunity to legitimize their experience as classroom teachers, and new teachers are impressed that the support teachers can really teach. The support teacher and the graduate intern also study teaching together. In study groups a small group of new teachers meet with one clinical-support teacher after school to talk about specific aspects of teaching. They are constantly reflecting and analyzing teaching together.

The most-often-mentioned strength of our program by beginning teachers is the nonthreatening feedback about their teaching which they receive. If induction programs offer unconditional, interpersonal support, they improve the quality of life for beginning teachers. This is an important point since so many first-year teachers leave the profession. (Feiman-Nemser, 1988a, pp. 14–15)

Toledo Program

Feiman-Nemser (1988b) relates that the Toledo Internship Program was inaugurated in 1981. All new teachers to the system are assigned a consulting teacher whose role is both to evaluate and to support them in the classroom during the first year of service in the school system. The program was initiated by the teachers' union because most of the first-year teachers in the Toledo schools were poorly prepared in classroom management. The consulting teachers are chosen based on recommendations of school administrators and their own teaching colleagues. They serve for a three-year term.

Each consulting teacher is assigned seven to ten interns in the same certification area/level. These mentors observe the interns at least once every two weeks. Each observation is followed by a conference with the beginning teacher on what worked and did not work in the class lesson observed. Discussion often focuses on classroom management and teaching techniques. In addition, consulting teachers offer information to the interns on how the system works and may run workshops on assertiveness training for newcomers. Finally, consultants can arrange for beginners to observe other veteran teachers in the classroom.

The principal task of the consulting teacher is to recommend to an Intern Review Board made up of teachers and administrators whether the new teacher should be given a second one-year contract. Consequently, consulting teachers take "a fairly direct approach, zeroing in on problems and letting interns know where they stand right from the start" (Feiman-Nemser, 1988b, p. 96).

Consulting teachers do not espouse any particular view of classroom teaching. Rather than advocate their ways of teaching, the consultants are asked to "cultivate the strengths of their interns and to present alternatives" (Feiman-Nemser, 1988b, pp. 98–99). Good teaching, however, is associated with good classroom management. As a consulting teacher expressed it, "If they cannot manage a class, they cannot teach" (p. 99).

According to Dal Lawrence, President of the Toledo Federation of Teachers and Chairman of the Intern Review Board of the Toledo Internship Program:

The program works exactly the way it was designed to work when it was started eight years ago and it works well. Management's happy with it and we're happy with it. It screens out those people who show little aptitude for the classroom and gets them professional help. It has accomplished the other important thing of getting teachers in Toledo to buy into their responsibility for performance and excellence and to see that it's part of the process of building a profession. This has to be done if we're going to turn around public schools in this country. (Feiman-Nemser, 1988a, pp. 18–19)

Comparison of the Programs

The two mentorship programs have, of course, different substantive goals: the Albuquerque program's aim is to produce reflective teachers who will change the status quo, and the Toledo program's principal purpose is to help new teachers deal with the existing realities in urban schools. However, both programs work to create a greater sense of community between younger and older professionals who increasingly share a commitment to improving teaching in their schools. As Thelen (1973) states, "As a moral community, a profession is composed of people who think they are professionals and who seek, through the practical inquiry of their lives, both alone and together, to clarify and live up to what they mean by being a professional" (pp. 200–201). The two induction models are essential first steps in beginning a dialogue between and among teachers that helps deepen a sense of professional identity in their school communities. Only by creating an informed view of professionalism in the schools, as Buchmann (1986) points out, can the "ethos of individualism, conservatism and presentism" be overcome (p. 61). She argues:

Individual and collective learning in the teaching profession depend, in particular, on norms of collegiality and experimentation. Norms of collegiality can reduce workplace isolation and help develop an orientation toward the teaching role. Norms of experimentation are based on a conviction that teaching can always be better than it is. If it is expected that teachers test their beliefs and practices, schools can be places where students and teachers learn. (p. 65)

The Albuquerque and Toledo mentorship programs provide one base—one part of the foundation—for the development of appropriate norms of collegiality and experimentation in schools.

In a practical sense, what is critical to the success of both programs is that mentor teachers have the time, training, and resources to help their new colleagues in the classroom. In their roles, they also have the opportunity to renew themselves as well. Through their interactions with educators new to the field they gain new insights into their own teaching and the teaching process in general.

There are, of course, certain disadvantages both programs must constantly work to overcome. First, because the intern program is mandatory and mentors are assigned to first-year teachers, there is the potential problem of mismatch. Not all first-year teachers will relate equally well to their mentors. Conflicts over personality differences will be inevitable. Second, given the number of interns the mentor teacher in either program must work with, close personal relationships are not likely to develop with all or even a majority of interns. Common sense suggests that a trusting and effective relationship between a mentor and a beginning teacher evolves from mutual respect and personal commitment to each other. In this light, Phillips's discussion (cited in Gray & Gray, 1985) of the difference between "primary" and "secondary" mentors is relevant.

> The former have greater impact because they stick their necks out for their protégés, share power and expertise, give a personal blessing, and take a personal interest in the protégé's career and personal well-being; the latter show much less personal caring for the protége, functioning in a business-like manner. (p. 38)

It is difficult to see how in either program the support or consulting teacher can always be the primary mentor, since a one-on-one relationship with all those mentored is not feasible. At times, these experienced teachers will end up as secondary mentors who will have less influence on the beginning teacher than was hoped for or anticipated.

A third disadvantage is that both the clinical-support teachers and the consulting teachers are removed from all substantive classroom teaching responsibilities. It is one thing to give advice or to team teach on occasion in the beginner's class. It is quite another to be working daily in the "trenches" and encountering many of the same problems the new teacher is facing in the classroom. Further, removing teachers from the classroom may help promote a career ladder in public school teaching, but it also creates a new layer to the hierarchy in the school, with the regular classroom teacher still remaining at the bottom of the pyramid.

MENTORING OF BEGINNERS

While none of the beginners in the study were involved in a highly structured mentorship program like the Albuquerque or Toledo programs, many of the schools in the study provided buddy teachers for the beginning teachers. Most of these mentoring arrangements were voluntary and unstructured—depending on the goodwill and commitment of both the beginner and the experienced teacher. In other schools where no formal arrangements existed, as in the past, experienced teachers sometimes took the newcomers under their wings and provided emotional support and pedagogical advice. Also, in several of the middle schools, beginning teachers were part of an interdisciplinary teaching team. These beginners had an opportunity to plan and interact with veteran teachers in developing and implementing their curriculum. All of these beginning teachers welcomed this formal or informal help provided by the older teachers.

Here are the perspectives of three beginning social studies teachers who had mentors and one social studies teacher who had neither an assigned nor an informal mentor.

First-year Rural Middle School Teacher
(with an assigned mentor)

My mentor's been incredibly helpful because this was his course for several years. He has been very helpful in suggesting activities. He's very easy to talk to about things that go on in school—like school politics and who to see about what. It's funny, because I always see him when I need him. He just knows to pop down about two weeks before Christmas and say: "Are you still alive down here?" And the first day back after Christmas, he came down and said: "You're no longer a rookie." He's very supportive in terms of morale, resources— both human and material stuff.

Second-year Rural High School Teacher
(with multiple mentors)

I'm very, very lucky, this department looked after me amazingly well. I had mentors for every different thing. I did not have one person I could go to for everything. I did end up with a mentor who had a radically different teaching style from mine but he was just a godsend because I was teaching stuff that I had never even learned. At other times, I had teachers I could go to for advice about classroom management—lots of different teachers I could talk to. The head of my department is a guardian angel. Somewhere within the first month of teaching, I called him up crying hysterically and said, "You better talk fast because I'm quitting teaching now!" And he was so kind. He sat on the phone and talked to me. He has lots of ideas for lots of things. He told me again and again: "You know, a billion people in China really don't care if you blew that class—it's okay."

First-year Middle School Teacher in Urban Experimental School
(with two mentors)

I have two mentors. They're infinite in their ability to help me because I can always bounce ideas off them, and I can always get myself redirected and refocused. More important, these teachers are helping me to develop my own theories on education. Helping me to see the big picture of pedagogy and methodology. I need to see the things in their larger forms, and then I can bring them down and shape them into what I can do in my classroom. But if I don't get the big stuff, then for me to own it—forget it. I can never do it. I can do all the specific tests you want me to do but I want to know why I'm doing it. That's where they both help.

First-year Suburban High School Teacher
(without a mentor)

I probably wish I had one here—like yourself. Just sitting in a classroom and giving constructive compliments or criticism. You know—"jeez, that one worked well. I thought the kids really responded, or I thought you may have been a little confusing at this point." It's almost like I'm left to evaluate myself and sometimes I don't think that's such a good idea. There are days that go by and I don't think I learn anything about my teaching, and that's too bad. I wish I had someone.

From these "testimonies," it is clear that mentors perform and can play a significant role in the professional lives of beginning teachers. As can be seen, the mentor does provide "moral support, guidance and feedback" to the beginning teacher (Sacks & Brady, 1985). Mentors are also extremely helpful in explaining school procedures and routines that are initially puzzling to many novices. As James Crawford-Williams reports about his mentor:

It was incredible to have him tell me how things worked with students and with the administrative stuff. This is stuff I want to push away, to brush away. He told me how to do that stuff. So personally, I couldn't have had a better mentor. He saw what my weakness was and attempted to address it. I knew that if something needed to be picked up, he was there.

For the four teachers in the case studies, perhaps the most important function a mentor plays is that of a role model. Both Maria Fernandez and Wendy Light discuss how experienced teachers helped provide them inspiration as well as models of good practice. Maria states:

I loved working with my department chair. Probably of all of the people at the school, he was most influential. I wanted to be a teacher like him. He is an easy-going, unassuming kind of guy, but still has an inner strength that exuded power. He didn't need to be yelling or raising his voice to get students to do things.

Wendy commented in a similar way in regard to her mentor.

My informal mentor was most valuable to me as a role model. I like the way she interacted with the students and her undying positive attitude. She's just a very positive person, and I think most people at my school would probably agree with that description of her. I just felt comfortable going in and saying, "Oh, I had the worst time with so-and-so." She'd say, "Well, maybe you could try this, and, hey, don't worry about it, it happens."

For several beginners, the mentor–protégé relationship is also a two-way street that often leads to real friendship and trust. As Wendy explains, "The other thing I like about her is that she'd value my opinion. She's quite a bit older than I and she'd come and ask me things, too. I don't think a lot of teachers do that and we built a kind of little relationship because of that." Elizabeth Alberto, too, speaks of her relationship with her informal mentor as special. She says, "From the beginning, my mentor was always there to offer advice, materials, and ideas. My mentor is the one who is my best friend and to whom I would turn in any situation."

Mentors are important to many beginners in their initial year of teaching. But what of the longer-term perspective? How lasting is the significance of mentors to veteran teachers and administrators who had a mentor when they first started teaching? In the past, many beginning teachers had buddy teachers who mentored them informally. Often the department chair fulfilled this function. The mentors of James, Elizabeth, and Wendy all felt that having had a more experienced teacher as a mentor during their first year of teaching was vital to their development and growing sense of professionalism. They speak of former mentors vividly and enthusiastically. For example, Elizabeth's informal mentor said that her most valuable mentor was her department chair, who built up her self-confidence and self-esteem: "Whenever my chair came in to observe a class, always, there was a list of positive things. No matter how badly you did something, she'd find something positive. She'd start with the positive and work on the negative."

Wendy's department chair had a similar experience with his mentor, who provided emotional support as well as helping him establish roots and a sense of belonging. He says:

My first department head was very supportive to talk to, we went out socially, we had dinner together. We would talk during the school day. If I had a problem I could go to him. He was almost like a brother, a surrogate-father type. He was not that much older than me but he had so much experience in education. I felt comfortable with him around. He made me feel that I belonged.

Wendy's informal mentor thought her department chair also served as a mentor to her. She states, "I went to her readily when I had problems and she helped." Some experienced teachers also view mentors who had a broad and deepening view of their discipline as important role models. Elizabeth's department chair said, "I admired teachers who always taught from a solid intellectual basis. I think to teach a language apart from teaching its culture and literature is a wasteland. You can teach language and still teach some beautiful poetry. Those who did so were the teachers I admired."

Mentors, of course, can play multiple roles, including exemplar, motivator, and friend, as well as helping the novice reflect substantively on the teaching experience. James Crawford-Williams's department chair mentions that her cooperating teacher performed all of these functions. Her mentor also assisted her during her first year of teaching, since she took a job at the high school where she had student-taught. She states:

It was not only his modeling with his teaching, but his clear caring for me and his willingness to spend incredible amounts of time talking to me about what I was going to do and what I had done—where I had succeeded and where I hadn't. He made clear the bigger picture of classroom teaching while always providing practical suggestions for improving my teaching. He is still my friend today.

Mentorship is vital for the mentor as well as the beginner. As Levinson (1978) makes clear:

Being a mentor with young adults is one of the most significant relationships available to a [person] in middle age. The distinctive satisfaction of the mentor lies in furthering the development of young men and women—facilitating their efforts to form and live out their Dreams, to lead better lives according to their own values and abilities.
    There is a measure of altruism in mentoring—a sense of meeting an obligation of doing something for another being. But much more than altruism is involved: The mentor is doing something for himself. He is making productive use of his own knowledge and skill in middle age. He is learning in ways not otherwise possible. He is maintaining his connec-

tion with the forces of youthful energy in the world and in himself. He needs the recipient of mentoring as much as the recipient needs him. It is time that this simple truth becomes more widely known. (p. 253)

The mentors in this study who were asked about the benefits mentoring had for them as professionals agreed in large measure with Levinson. Elizabeth Alberto's informal mentor remarked:

> For me, it reinforced a lot of what I believe in. I learn so much from Elizabeth all the time. To have someone with lots of energy and fresh ideas, it's such a boost. She has broadened my perspectives in so many ways. She is someone who is caring and who is willing to do the work and the extras. She has certainly helped to renew me.

Wendy's mentor has similar views. She says:

> I really enjoyed it. I got a great deal of pleasure from it. I got confirmation of my strengths as a teacher, and I got a friendship which I think is very important. I liked working with her because she was so good, and I was helpful to her in terms of materials and schedules. But she was also very helpful to me. She has strengths I don't have—her very high energy level and her determination to go out and do things. I did some things with her that I might not have done otherwise, such as school field trips.

James Crawford-Williams's mentor also believes it provides perspective and a shot in the arm. He says:

> It was very helpful to me because it reminded me of the way things were when I started. It also served to remind me where I may have slipped in the last couple of years, i.e., an extra review sheet that I could have passed out and didn't; or spending more time after school and being more available rather than stuck in my routine. The things that I let slide for a bit, I thought I'd better tighten up.

James's department chair feels she learns most about teaching by talking to newcomers about teaching and by discussing how "to help meet kids' needs with young people who care about it." Maria's buddy teacher also feels that a mentor helps you keep on top of teaching. He says, "There is a refreshment involved in mentoring. It forces you to re-examine what you are doing in a step-by-step fashion."

Finally, Wendy's department chair asserts:

It makes me feel valuable. I feel like I have something to contribute to her professionalism, her career. And vice versa is true as well. She can help me look at something in a different light. It's mainly the positive feeling that you get from being asked your opinion—that your opinion is valuable gives you a sense of well-being in the profession.

In brief, the mentorship of beginners in the study who had such a personal and professional relationship with their mentors seems to be helping break down the hands-off ethic in the school culture. Learning to teach may still be mainly an "independent study project" for beginners, but at least in some schools there is collegial support and concern, which makes a difference to beginners like Elizabeth and Wendy. In these two cases, the mentoring relationship is close to what Levinson (1978) talks about in his analysis as "good enough" mentoring relations. The newcomer "feels admiration, respect, appreciation, gratitude and love for the mentor. . . . The elder has qualities of character, expertise and understanding that the younger admires and wants to make part of himself" (p. 100). These mentoring relationships were formed voluntarily and grew in vitality and substance based on mutual interests and affiliations. In the case of Elizabeth and Wendy these mentoring relations were also not planned. Each had been assigned other mentors at the start of the school year. The informal mentoring by the two experienced women teachers facilitated the socialization of the two younger teachers to their teaching roles in and outside the classroom.

For the most part, the help new teachers such as Elizabeth, Wendy, James, and Maria receive from their veteran colleagues, while valuable, is informal, practical, and given upon request. As one first-year teacher put it when asked whether she had a mentor: "I sort of do. But they don't come and ask you what you need all the time. You have to go to them, which is a little different from having an actual mentor." And only in the instances of the beginner who teaches at the urban experimental school and CW's department chair, does there seem to be any dialogue between the beginning teachers and their more experienced colleagues about the substantive purposes of schooling and how the pedagogical innovations they undertake fit into the larger conceptual scheme. While "reflection" may be an overused term in current parlance in teacher education, most of the mentors do not act presently as catalysts for reflective thinking and the greater empowerment of the beginning teachers. The role they play is, of course, crucial and often fulfills the beginners' "felt needs." But it is the vision and the "big picture" that also need to be worried about in the real world of teaching. In Hannah Arendt's phrase, there is also a time to "stop-and-think" about practice (Schön, 1988, p. 29).

SUMMARY

Mentorship is an educational reform that is being implemented nation-wide and often has a significant and positive impact on the beginning teacher and his or her mentor. Developmentally, it can help younger novices begin to fulfill the Dream they want to realize as new professionals. The Dream has, in Levinson's (1978) words, "the quality of a vision, an imagined possibility that generates excitement and vitality." It may take many forms, including the heroic as well as the more ordinary, yet still "inspiring and sustaining" the vision of the "excellent craftsman" or craftswoman (p. 91). In mentoring, many experienced teachers, too, benefit by renewing and refreshing themselves through interaction with new and energetic colleagues.

Professionally, a certain form of mentorship has the catalytic power to help promote community and strengthen the norms of collegiality and experimentation in the school context. Thus it is an innovation that can help foster the improvement of teaching and encourage sustained faculty reflection. Yet, it cannot be done inexpensively. Moreover, new models of mentorship are needed that combine the advantages of voluntary and often ad hoc mentoring relationships established by like-minded experienced and inexperienced teachers, and more systematic but conceivably less personally significant mandated school-wide programs that reach all new teachers and provide them a shared perspective on teaching and opportunities for reflection on the bigger issues and concerns of classroom teachers. Such new reflective mentoring models, as outlined in Chapter 11, are both possible and within the financial means of most school systems committed to school restructuring and the greater empowerment of teachers.

CHAPTER 11

Conclusions

In this final chapter, a summary of findings is presented, followed by a set of recommendations for improving the first-year induction process of the beginning teacher. These recommendations help to address the need to attract and maintain in teaching more liberally educated and dynamic educators like those represented in the study. The proposed reforms also have implications for more experienced teachers as well as for the teaching profession in general.

SUMMARY OF FINDINGS

In this study, the data suggest that this group of bright and articulate beginning teachers are hard-working and caring young professionals who have made at least provisional commitments to careers in teaching and serving the public interest. They are pragmatic idealists who express a high regard for both the subject matter and their students. Often their principal reasons for teaching center on commitment and service: to working with the young in a special calling that requires sacrifice and dedication. As reflected in the four case studies, their mentors often praise them for their high standards; their subject-matter competence; their ability to solve problems of classroom practice quickly and effectively; their energetic level of initiative, involvement, and follow-through; and their willingness to go the extra mile in helping their students, their colleagues, and their schools. While this general set of leadership and professional qualities is not unique to this study group, these personal attributes often make these beginners special in the eyes of their colleagues and school administrators.

During the first years of teaching, they are developing self-constructed professional identities that are often based on realistic yet optimistic assessments of schools and how they work as complex bureaucratic institutions. In learning to teach and adapt to pluralistic school cultures, the beginners

144

often adopt an eclectic, pragmatic approach to teaching that combines both progressive and traditional views about the nature of students and the teaching and learning processes. While their criteria of good teaching vary, they usually center on helping students become autonomous learners while making learning enjoyable and interesting. They use a variety of teaching approaches to execute their vision of effective teaching in the classroom. Because of their own character and their prior work in the schools as observers, tutors, and student teachers—field experiences that they most often rate as good to excellent—they suffer little reality shock when they begin full-time secondary school teaching. Like other new professionals, they, of course, confront problems, dilemmas, and a great deal of role strain as they "learn the ropes." Consequently, job stress is part of their daily reality. They work long hours, including weekends, and at times feel overwhelmed and exhausted, particularly during the first half of the academic year. However, through hard work and effort, the beginners in the study manage to stay on their feet and get on top of teaching by the end of the first year on the job.

Like veteran teachers in their schools, they face the challenge of dealing with the interrelated problems of maintaining classroom discipline and student motivation in a compulsory school environment. Normally, they are tested early and frequently by students. Initially, discipline may be a major problem for some new teachers. However, for the majority of beginners in this study, classroom discipline as well as most other first-year teaching problems, such as motivation or dealing with slow learners, are perceived as moderately serious but not significant concerns. These problems appear manageable to most of these beginners.

The mentorship of teachers by their colleagues or immediate supervisors was considered valuable by both those beginning and experienced teachers in this study who engaged in some form of mentoring relationship. Typically, the mentor teachers provide specific advice on the curriculum and on the nitty-gritty aspects of classroom teaching. They also offer moral support and friendship. At times, the mentoring grows into an authentic and highly nurturing relationship that promotes psychological development of the newcomer as well as the new teacher's socialization into the school community. It also has positive effects and benefits for experienced teachers. In most cases, the help beginners receive meets their felt and immediate needs, but the interaction does not often foster substantive reflection about teaching and the profession itself.

Five substantive areas of concern have been identified that need to be addressed by school administrators and experienced teachers in helping beginning teachers adjust to and grow in their role as teachers: working out their classroom authority role; gaining teaching competence in the subject matter; maintaining a high sense of efficacy in reaching and teaching adolescents most at risk; gaining or refining their moral decision-making skills; and becoming more reflective practitioners of their new craft. Each of these concerns is briefly discussed below.

1. *Classroom Authority.* Developing a classroom teacher persona is often more difficult than anticipated by first-year teachers. Learning to exercise adult authority is a complex process that involves coming to understand the context and what is expected of teachers and students in a particular school culture. But it is, of course, affected by one's view of education and of human nature. When these variables are in conflict or at least initially out of "sync," a beginning teacher is likely to feel conflicted and confused. Because of the uncertainty and variability of the classroom, even when the two sets of variables are more or less compatible, teachers may also confront situations in which they are unsure of their authority. The calculus of interactions of the secondary classroom requires that new teachers develop as clear a sense of their classroom role as practicable. This process can be helped by dialogue and reflection.

2. *Teaching Competence.* New teachers confront the perplexing problem of determining "what is worth knowing" while at the same time justifying the subject matter to students. Simultaneously, they must "psychologize" or make meaningful the content, often while learning it for the first time. Beginning teachers clearly need help in thinking through their objectives and translating the facts and concepts of the curriculum in ways that are relevant and significant to adolescents. Veteran teachers' sharing of materials is not sufficient. First-year teachers need to gain a deeper understanding of the larger picture and how the pieces fit together to make a mosaic worth contemplating by their students. Again, sustained conversation with colleagues will be helpful to new teachers in gaining true teaching competence in the subject matter sooner.

3. *Reaching Adolescents at Risk.* At the start of first-year teaching, most new teachers are committed to helping the adolescents most in need of help in school. Often, these students are difficult to handle and may be "turned off" from school or hold a different work ethic from that of beginning teachers. Initially, beginning teachers often confront failure when working with these students. Their high sense of personal efficacy—feeling able to make a difference—may diminish. They may become disillusioned and discouraged. If as a result they develop a low sense of personal efficacy—feeling that nothing can be done by them to help these adolescents—then they and their students lose. Veteran teachers who have maintained a high sense of efficacy to make a difference in the lives of these youngsters

have an important role to play in the professional development of the beginning teachers. The experienced teachers need to work with the beginning teachers to help them deal with the inevitable defeats and accompanying sense of failure, and to help these new professionals succeed in teaching these at-risk students effectively.

4. *Moral Decision Making.* As the teaching dilemmas in the study reveal, beginning teachers often confront tough choices that test their character as well as their ability to act reasonably and compassionately in a crisis. The situations they face in the classroom and the school are often different from those they have encountered in the past. Whether the problem relates to unacceptable classroom behavior or deciding whether to flunk a student, first- or second-year teachers are often unsure of the soundness or appropriateness of their decisions. Of course, the neophyte must be allowed to make mistakes and to learn from errors of judgment. There are areas of uncertainty where there are no right answers or situations where there are only bad choices. Yet, a "wise head" can help young professionals avoid or repair some mistakes that hurt their relationships with their students or with the larger school community. After all, teaching is a moral craft as much as it is an intellectual enterprise. As Robert Coles (1987) argues, the development of moral competence is just as important as the acquisition of intellectual competencies.

5. *On-the-Run Teaching.* Because of the hectic nature of the school day, beginning teachers do not have adequate time to reflect on their practice or to revise plans for more effective instruction. It is often "catch as catch can" during the school day. The norms of the teaching profession as well as other professions work against assessing, revising, and improving one's daily on-the-job performance. There is just too much more to be done. Yet, reflection-on-practice is the mark of professionalism and the principal way to bring about improvement in teaching. Beginning teachers need to be encouraged and given time to reflect on practice and to consider how good practice can be informed by good theory.

On the whole, the beginning teachers in this study successfully negotiated their first year of teaching. They not only survived but survived with dignity, often exceeding their expectations for the first year of teaching. As the four case studies illustrate, beginners often found teaching intrinsically rewarding, emphasizing foremost their personal relationship and successes with students.

They were also challenged and tested. While they learned from these experiences, the areas of concern that have been identified suggest ways in which the first-year induction process can be improved through greater collegiality and mentorship in schools.

RECOMMENDATIONS

Cogan's (1973) observations about inadequate supervision "Teachers are better left alone than tampered with" (p. 15), are on target. His main point, however, is that "an important part of the delay and failure characteristic of innovation in American schools is attributed to the lack of trained in-class support" (p. 5). The problem, then, is to provide the right kind of support to newly hired teachers in their classrooms. It requires collegial support that fosters personal and professional growth, while not tampering with but rather promoting the beginner's autonomy in the classroom. It is no simple task. Mencken's aphorism (cited in Egar, 1968) holds true particularly in the culture of the schools: "There's always an easy solution to every human problem — neat, plausible and wrong" (p. 751). Thus in presenting any set of recommendations to improve the first-year induction process, care must be taken not to provide simply a list of quick fixes or doable reforms. It just is not that simple.

Findings from this study suggest that the right kind of support for first-year teachers must center on a mentoring system that fosters their developmental and professional growth as well as on that of their experienced colleagues. Erikson's (1959) concept of mutuality applies: A person at whatever stage of the life cycle is both shaped and helps shape the development of the other generations. In the specific context of the workplace, Levinson (1978), too, emphasizes the importance of the mentoring relationship for both the mentor and the inexperienced associate. Vailliant's (1977) notion of generativity — "responsibility for the growth, leadership and well-being of one's fellow creatures" — is at the heart of a mature nurturing relationship (p. 202). The younger professionals want increasingly to make a difference. The veteran teachers need to continue to feel that they do make a difference in the lives of others. But in Gilligan's (1982) terms, such mentoring for most women and many men as well must be based on the "ethic of nurturance, responsibility and care" (p. 159), if we wish a more complete and enduring generative relationship to exist among teachers of different sexes, ages, and perspectives.

While the psychological development of the new teacher and the experienced teacher is crucial to a sustained mentoring relationship, professional growth is, of course, the central concern. Professional growth, however, implies more than learning the ropes and becoming "street wise" in the world of teaching. It involves becoming reflective and critical of one's own classroom practice, and helping to develop and implement standards of good teaching in schools.

Reflection-on-practice, however, needs to be more precisely defined and its parameters marked out. As Kennedy (1989a) relates, what is hoped is that teachers will by "reflecting on their own or on others' experiences develop a thoughtful, situation-based sense of what constitutes good practice" (p. 2). In the final analysis, reflection helps inform the teacher's working knowledge—"the knowledge at the fingertips, the organized body of ideas, beliefs, experiences, and values that provide the basis for decisions" (p. 5). In an interview by Kennedy (1989b), Kenneth Zeichner discusses three forms of reflection that need to be engaged in by the mentor and the beginner. He states:

> The first form of reflection is technical or instrumental: Teachers reflect about the best way to get somewhere when the "somewhere" is already determined. The second form is practical reflection: Teachers deliberate both about the means and about their purposes. "Are kids learning? What are they learning? and Is this what they should be learning?"
>
> There's another kind of reflection that we're also concerned about, critical reflection. Critical reflection happens when teachers raise issues that have to do with ethical and moral dimensions of teaching that aren't necessarily explicit within the other forms of reflection. It goes beyond asking, "What are kids learning and should they be learning that?" Instead, critical reflection raises questions related to moral dimensions of teaching, such as what kinds of things are particular children and groups of children learning. [For example,] it could be something about what are boys and girls learning in mathematics class—both the math and some affective things as well. (pp. 15–16)

Providing beginning teachers with opportunities for these various ways of reflecting on practice may at first be difficult to achieve in schools, with their present organizational structure and ethos. At least initially, teacher educators from the university or local college may be helpful in providing insight into the reflective teacher literature and how these three forms of reflection may take place in the mentoring relationship. But more important, higher education professionals need to engage in a sustained conversation with school practitioners about the changing nature of classroom teaching and good practice. In the process, teacher educators and classroom teachers will learn from each other in ways that should improve both preservice and inservice education.

But such collaboration is not enough. Helping beginners learn to teach in ways that foster reflection and collegiality requires major reform of most schools' induction practices. In my view, a comprehensive induction program should include: (1) a first-year internship, (2) a senior teacher committee, and (3) core workshops. The first-year internship will provide beginners with the nurturing support of an experienced colleague and time to reflect on practice. Colleagues within the teaching field and the school would also serve as secondary mentors to the novice teacher. While a principal mentor should be assigned to each new teacher, multiple mentors are needed to provide alternative pathways of support so that an optimum amount of choice and voluntary collaboration is provided to the beginner in the mentoring process.

A committee of senior teachers should also be established whose responsibility would be to help set up and maintain a mentorship program and to evaluate the beginning teachers in the light of standards of good practice as articulated by the teaching staff and school administration. Finally, new teachers should complete certain workshop modules in teaching and classroom management techniques that are generally agreed to be important for successful classroom teaching in the school. In addition, all faculty need orientation workshops on the establishment of an effective mentoring program in the school. Each recommendation is outlined in greater detail below.

First-Year Internship

The core recommendation is consistent with many others proposed or implemented over the last 20 or so years: a first-year teaching internship—one with a teaching load reduced by one class for the beginning teacher and a comparably reduced load for an experienced mentor teacher who will work closely with the novice teacher in the classroom.

A similar recommendation was made by the National Association of Secondary School Principals in 1968 (Hunt, 1968). The British are now experimenting with such induction programs (Feiman-Nemser, 1983, p. 160). And a second-year teacher in this study recommends something similar: "one year of full-time teaching, working closely with an experienced mentor teacher who receives remuneration for his/her time and effort."

Given the complexity of teaching, it is important that first-year teachers have available "multiple mentors" to help guide and evaluate their progress. Because of the eclectic nature of secondary school teaching, it is particularly desirable that beginning teachers have the opportunity and option of drawing upon the diverse strengths of their colleagues and school administrators in gaining greater teaching competence and a fuller sense of the teaching and learning processes in their school context.

The principal mentor should be a regular classroom teacher who teaches in the same field and who has fine teaching and interpersonal skills and high standards of performance for all students. This experienced teacher would have the major responsibility for assisting the new teacher in learning to teach. As a "good enough" mentor, he or she would act as an advocate and friend, providing "constructive advice and criticism" but not having any formal supervisory duties that might interfere in establishing a close and personal relationship with the novice teacher. Chief responsibilities of the principal mentor would be to help new teachers reflect on good practice, to acquire or refine essential teaching skills, and to assist the newcomer in planning and implementing a curriculum that was relevant and meaningful for students. Finally, the beginner would have the opportunity to observe the mentor teacher in the classroom and might be teamed with the mentor in teaching one or two classes.

Secondary mentors would play a role in helping in each of these areas, particularly providing curricular ideas and pedagogical suggestions for what works in the classroom for students at risk. As is bound to happen, such as in the cases of Elizabeth Alberto and Wendy Light, a secondary mentor may become the primary mentor of the beginning teacher. While awkward, a change of principal mentors can be worked out at the end of the first academic semester to accommodate the development of a more authentic and valuable mentoring relationship. In that case, the new principal mentor would reduce his or her teaching load by one course, and the former mentor would correspondingly be expected to increase his or her teaching load by a course or assume additional teaching and nonteaching duties.

Senior Teacher Committee

Along with the school administration, the senior teacher committee would set up and coordinate the mentoring program, and help fulfill the monitoring and evaluation function. Specifically, the committee would provide orientation and ongoing workshops on the mentoring process for beginners and veteran staff. Moreover, the senior teacher committee would help to determine and uphold the standards of good practice in the particular school. It is not envisioned that the committee's primary task would be to make pronouncements and mandate certain practices. Rather, the committee's role would be to support reflection-on-action in the classroom and to build consensus among the staff about good teaching in the school and the importance of mentoring the next generation of teachers. The committee members should, of course, be informed by the latest research on teacher effectiveness and also by their colleagues' views of good teaching and the recognition that there often is no single best way.

Before the senior teacher committee could be established, the school board and school administration would need to agree to a new evaluation procedure that included senior teachers as evaluators. There would also be a need to recognize that the assessment of teachers in different subject areas often requires different procedures and criteria of evaluation.

The teachers who sit on the committee should be senior teachers elected by the faculty and eventually, it is hoped, should include at least one or two past mentors who fully understand the mentorship process. The senior teacher committee members, too, will need to have released time from their classes to perform their various duties. As respected peers, their role would be to provide perspective and more objective and impartial evaluation, and to see to it that beginners have school-wide opportunities to reflect on their teaching. At times, helping make tough decisions about reappointment will, of course, be difficult. And attempting to forge consensus among teachers who value their individualism and classroom prerogatives will also be frustrating. Yet, the senior teacher committee will have the unique opportunity to help make teaching a more autonomous and respected profession.

This committee of "wise heads" might also include as a consultant a teacher educator from the beginning teacher's college or university or from the local area. When appropriate, this individual would provide additional training or act as a facilitator in making available to the beginning teachers opportunities and resources at the university. This is the kind of college–school partnership that makes the most sense. It breaks down barriers between school and university and helps make both institutions of learning more accountable for their work in preparing and supporting beginning teachers.

Core Workshops

Two types of workshops are envisioned: orientation inservice meetings for all faculty on mentoring, and classroom management and innovative teaching methods seminars for beginning teachers. These various workshops would provide opportunity for reflection, the sharing of perspectives, and the building of a sense of professional community.

1. *Orientation.* Besides specific orientation sessions for beginners, all teachers within a school need to discuss the concept of mentorship and the roles of the principal and secondary mentors. The senior teacher committee would have the primary responsibility for implementing workshops for all teachers and for the principal mentor teachers as well. Workshop material such as Judith Shulman and Joel Colbert's *The Mentor Teacher Casebook* (1987) and the Evergreen Collegial Teacher Training Consortium's *The Mentor Teacher Handbook* (1987) are useful references. But these educational resources are only starting points. Over time, the teachers in the school must develop their own orientation programs based on their informed judgments and what works best in helping all teachers better mentor their colleagues. More specifically for the principal mentors, substantive

dialogue needs to take place around the need for beginning teachers to become more reflective practitioners of their craft.

2. *Classroom Teaching and Management Workshops.* One systemic problem of both preservice and inservice education must also be tackled. Not only are new teachers pretty much left to their own devices in the classroom, but they also often receive insufficient substantive training in classroom strategies and procedures that might make a difference. While they often are exposed to innovative teaching strategies in their preprofessional courses and inservice education, some of this information is not relevant until they attempt to implement innovations in their own classrooms. For example, they may have a one-day workshop on cooperative learning. It is then up to them to experiment with and adapt the new approach to learning in their classes. Initially, the innovation may or may not work for them. If not, the novice may not use the classroom technique again or may use it only as a diversion or change-of-pace activity, thus failing to capitalize on its full potential. In their work on the coaching of teaching, Joyce and Showers (1982) relate that acquiring a complex teaching skill requires many hours of practice before the teacher is competent and proficient in its employment. Under present conditions, few beginners on their own have the time or energy to undertake an "autotutorial."

The school faculty should decide what classroom procedures and techniques they feel a beginning teacher should gain competence in during the first year of teaching. The focus may be on issues of classroom management, the process approach to writing, interdisciplinary programs, or cooperative learning activities that promote student learning, particularly with the most difficult-to-handle adolescents. An effective workshop program series, of course, needs to be devised and implemented by the senior teacher committee, perhaps with the help of a teacher educator consultant or other professionals at a higher education institution. With the proper mentorship available, including observing mentor teachers practicing the technique, the beginner would be required to complete satisfactorily these 10- to 15-hour training modules by the end of the academic year. They would, of course, be evaluated by the senior teacher committee on how well they performed the classroom procedures or skills by actual classroom observation over time and, when necessary, with different classes or ability groupings.

Summary

The advantages of this induction program focusing on reflective mentoring are threefold. It makes the induction of the beginning teacher a truly collegial and collaborative enterprise of the school faculty and hopefully the teacher education institution. It makes assessment both more realistic and more systematic. And it promotes the development of standards of practice that are owned by the teaching faculty, and not just imposed externally by the state or some other distant bureaucracy.

There is perhaps a fourth advantage. The multiple mentorship system with its substantive workshop component may be an essential ingredient in the proposed National Board for Professional Standards. Testing professional competence can validly be done only in context. There must be testimony from colleagues as well as on-site observation to verify that an educator is meeting "high standards of what teachers need to know and be able to do" (Carnegie Forum on Education and the Economy, 1986, p. 55). In short, "to certify [as] teachers who meet those standards" requires not just passing a test and presenting a portfolio but also demonstrating over time good practice of the craft as regarded by "significant others" in the school environment (p. 55). That's what makes a difference.

I recognize the problems of the multiple mentorship induction program. Critics will raise objections: It's too costly; there are better ways to use scarce resources; it's too bureaucratic—another "hurdle" for the beginning teacher to jump; it doesn't go far enough to ensure "quality control"; there may result "Mickey Mouse" workshop modules worse than those suffered through by the beginning teacher in the preparation program; finally, it's still too sketchy—more details are needed to understand fully how it would work in practice. Yet, the need is critical. A pilot program in several schools to see how well the multiple, reflective mentorship "stuff" works in the real world of teaching is worth the risk. It seems to me to be the right kind of support that beginning teachers should have to help them not only survive but develop as effective teachers during their first year in the profession.

There are, of course, other recommendations that could be made to improve the beginning teaching experience. From this study, there are a number of substantive issues about teacher-as-classroom-authority, methods and criteria of grading, and the teaching of adolescents most at risk that should be talked about and analyzed by the beginner and the mentors and supervisors in seminars and workshops. And there are other things that I have not mentioned in the hope that William James (1918) is right: "The art of being wise is the art of knowing what to overlook" (p. 369). However, the one thing not to overlook is that capable and idealistic men and women will be drawn to and remain in teaching when their personal Dreams for themselves as professionals and their vision of their craft as a respected and dynamic profession can be satisfied. To fulfill this mosaic of Dreams and visions, we need school reform such as reflective mentoring that encourages good classroom teaching. In the historian Page Smith's (1990) parting words:

> We need to establish new rhythms, new ways of learning, new ways of celebrating. We need alternation and alternatives; action and response; freshening of the spirit and lightening of the mind. We need to teach. (p. 222)

To teach in this manner requires, in Buchmann's (1986) terms, collegiality and experimentation. These human endeavors are also key to the development of teaching as a profession. As has been noted, in experimenting and extending the frontiers of knowledge of teaching, young professionals often have as important a role to play as experienced teachers. Clearly, in pioneering and creating new forms of collegial relationships in the school such as mentoring, the rookie teacher will be at the center of and central to building a new professional identity for teachers of all ages and experience.

APPENDIX

Other Critical Moments in the Cycle of Teaching

Figure 1. Time of First Teaching Triumph

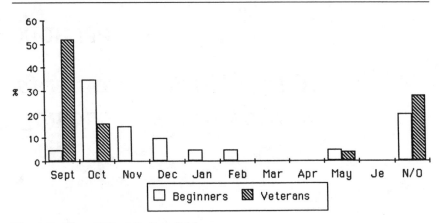

Figure 2. Time of Most Serious Crisis

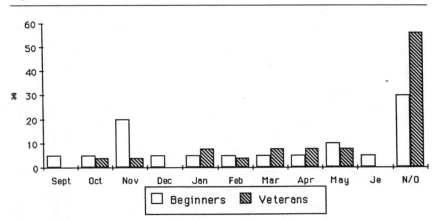

Figure 3. First Time Tested by Student

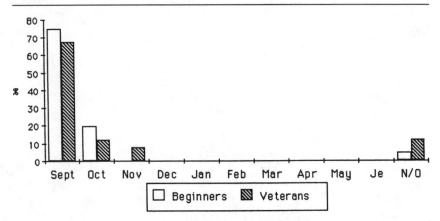

Figure 4. First Compliment from a Student

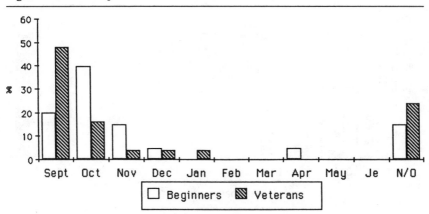

Figure 5. First Time Student "Got to You"

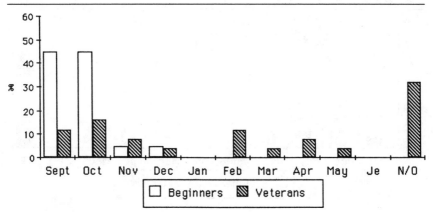

Figure 6. First Time a Class "Got to You"

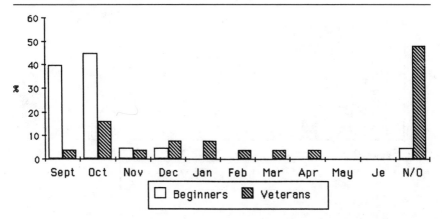

Figure 7. First Time Gave Student Detention

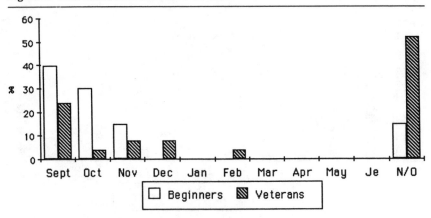

Figure 8. First Time Sent Student Out of Class

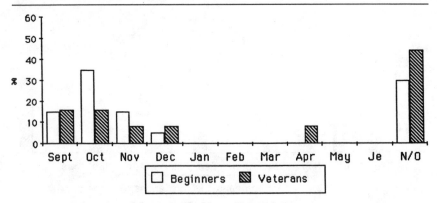

Figure 9. First Time Talked to Principal About Discipline Problem

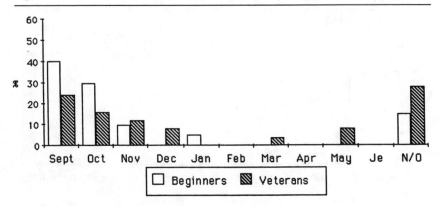

Figure 10. Time Discipline a Serious Problem

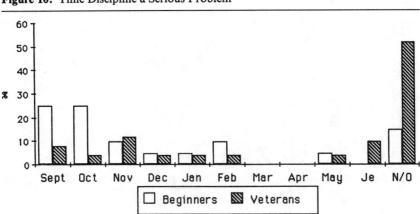

Figure 11. First Time: Why Did I Get into This?

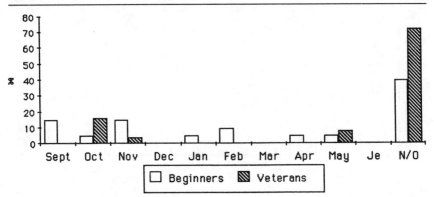

Figure 12. First Monday Didn't Want to Get Out of Bed

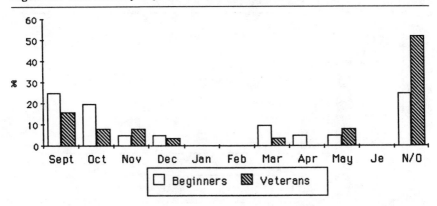

Figure 13. Time Got to Know Most Students

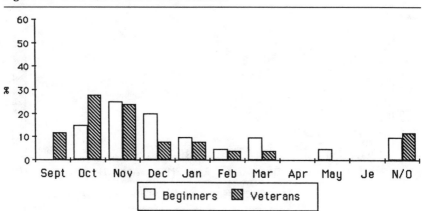

Figure 14. Time Felt on Top of Teaching

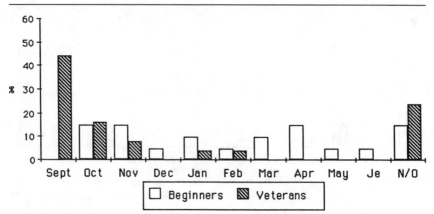

Figure 15. First Time Talked to a Parent About a Student

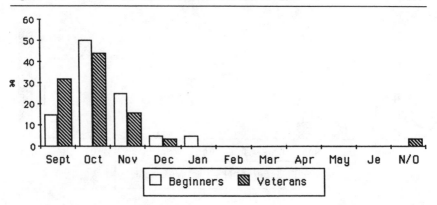

References

Ashton, P., & Webb, R. B. (1986). *Making a difference: Teachers' sense of efficacy and student achievement*. New York: Longman.

Bailyn, B. (1960). *Education in the forming of American society*. New York: Vintage Books.

Barr, R., & Dreeben, R. (1980). *How schools work*. Chicago: University of Chicago Press.

Becker, H. S., Geer, B., Hughes, E. C., & Strauss, A. L. (1961). *Boys in white: Student culture in medical school*. Chicago: University of Chicago Press.

Berliner, D. C. (1988, October). *Implications of studies of expertise in pedagogy for teacher education and evaluation*. Paper presented at Educational Testing Service Invitational Conference, New York.

Berman, P., McLaughlin, M., Bass, G., Pauly, E., & Zeller, G. (1977). *Federal programs for supporting educational change: Vol. 7. Factors affecting implementation and continuation*. Santa Monica, CA: Rand Corporation. (ERIC Document Reproduction Service No. ED 140 432)

Bloom, A. (Trans.). (1968). *The republic of Plato*. New York: Basic Books.

Bolt, R. (1962). *A man for all seasons*. New York: Vintage Books.

Buchmann, M. (1986). Role over person: Legitimacy and authenticity in teaching. In M. Ben-Peretz, R. Bromme, & R. Halkes (Eds.), *Advances of research in teacher thinking* (pp. 55–69). Berwyn, PA: Swets North America Inc.

Burden, P. (1981, November). *Teachers' perception of their personal and professional development*. Paper presented at the annual meeting of the Midwestern Educational Research Association, Des Moines, IA.

California State Department of Education. (1983). *California mentor teacher program*. Sacramento: California Department of Education. (ERIC Document Research Study No. ED 241 473)

Carnegie Forum on Education and the Economy. (1986). *A nation prepared: Teachers for the 21st century: The report of the task force on teaching as a profession*. Washington, DC: Author.

Coalition of Essential Schools. (1991). *Prospectus: Coalition of essential schools*. Providence, RI: Author.

Coates, T. J., & Thorensen, C. E. (1976). Teacher anxiety: A review with recommendation. *Review of Educational Research, 46*, 159–184.

Cogan, M. L. (1973). *Clinical supervision*. Boston: Houghton Mifflin.

Coles, R. (1986). *The moral life of children*. Boston: Atlantic Monthly Press.

Coles, R. (1987). Educating for a moral life. *Harvard Education Review, 57*(2), 193–195.

Coles, R. (1990, September). Teachers who made a difference. *Instructor, 59*, 58–59.

Cronbach, L. J. (1990). *Essentials of psychological testing* (5th ed.). New York: Harper & Row.

Dewey, J. (1938). *Logic: The theory of inquiry*. New York: Holt, Rinehart and Winston.

Dewey, J. (1974). The child and the curriculum. In R. D. Archambault (Ed.), *John Dewey on education* (pp. 339–358). Chicago: University of Chicago Press.

Dickmeyer, N. (1989). Metaphor, models, and theory in education research. *Teachers College Record, 91*, 151–160.

Doyle, W. (1977, November/December). Learning the classroom environment: An ecological analysis. *Journal of Teacher Education, 28*, 51–55.

Dunn, L. E. (1972). Problems encountered by Northwest State University secondary education graduates: A comparative study of problems of beginning and experienced teachers (Doctoral dissertation, Northwestern University of Louisiana, 1972). *Dissertation Abstracts International, 33*, 05–A.

Egar, E. (1968). *20,000 quips and quotes*. Garden City, NY: Doubleday.

Erikson, E. H. (1959). *Identity and the life cycle: Psychological issues*. New York: International Universities Press.

Erikson, E. H. (1963). Youth: Fidelity and diversity. In E. H. Erikson (Ed.), *The challenge of youth* (pp. 1–28). New York: Doubleday.

Erikson, E. H. (1964). *Insight and responsibility*. New York: Norton.

Erikson, E. H. (1968). *Identity: Youth and crisis*. New York: Norton.

Evergreen Collegial Teacher Training Consortium. (1987). *Mentor teacher handbook*. Vancouver, BC: Author.

Featherstone, J. (1988). A note on liberal learning. *NCRTE Colloquy, 2*(1), 1–8. East Lansing: Michigan State University.

Featherstone, J. (1989, August). Good instruction. *Instructor*, pp. 32–36.

Feiman-Nemser, S. (1983). Learning to teach. In L. S. Shulman & G. Sykes (Eds.), *Handbook of teaching and policy* (pp. 150–170). New York: Longman.

Feiman-Nemser, S. (Ed.). (1988a). Induction programs and the professionalization of teachers: Two views. *NCRTE Colloquy, 1*(2), 11–19. East Lansing: Michigan State University.

Feiman-Nemser, S. (1988b). Toledo schools/Toledo Federation of Teachers Toledo Internship Program site report. *Dialogues in teacher education* (Issue Paper 88-4), 95–106. East Lansing: Michigan State University.

Feiman-Nemser, S., & Buchmann, M. (1985). *The first year of teacher preparation: Transition to pedagogical thinking?* (Research Report Series No. 156). East Lansing: Michigan State University for Research in Teaching.

Floden, R. E., & Clark, C. M. (1988). Preparing teachers for uncertainty. *Teachers College Record, 89*(4), 505–524.

Fuller, F. F. (1969, March). Concerns of teachers: A developmental conceptualization. *American Educational Research Journal, 6*, 207–226.

Gay, P. (Trans.). (1963). *Voltaire's Candide*. New York: St. Martin's Press.

Gilligan, C. (1982). *In a different voice*. Cambridge, MA: Harvard University Press.

Goodlad, J. (1984). *A place called school*. New York: McGraw-Hill.

Goodlad, J. (1990). *Teachers for our nation's schools*. San Francisco: Jossey-Bass.

Gray, W. A., & Gray, M. M. (1985). Synthesis of research on mentoring beginning teachers. *Educational Leadership, 43*, 37–43.

Grossman, P. L., Wilson, S. M., & Shulman, L. S. (1989). Teachers of substance: Subject matter knowledge for teaching. In M. C. Reynolds (Ed.), *Knowledge base for the beginning teacher* (pp. 23–36). New York: Pergamon Press.

Gursky, D. (1990, June/July). A plan that works. *Teacher, 47*, 46–54.

Hammersley, M. (Ed.). (1986). *Controversies in classroom research*. Philadelphia: Open University Press.

Hennig, M., & Jardim, A. (1977). *The managerial woman*. Garden City, NY: Anchor Press/Doubleday.

Hunt, D. C. (1968). Teacher induction: An opportunity and a responsibility. *The Bulletin of the National Association of Secondary School Principals, 52*, 130–135.

Jackson, P. W. (1987). The future of teaching. In F. S. Bolin & J. M. Falk (Eds.), *Teacher renewal* (pp. 43–58). New York: Teachers College Press.

James, W. (1918). *Principles of psychology* (Vol. 2). New York: Henry Holt.

Johnson, J. S., Jr., & Associates. (1989). *Those who can*. Washington, DC: Association of American Colleges.

Joyce, B. A., & Showers, B. (1982). The coaching of teaching. *Educational Leadership, 40*, 445–455.

Keizer, G. (1988). *No place but here: A teacher's vocation in a rural community*. New York: Viking Press.

Kennedy, M. M. (1989a). Reflections and the problems of professional standards. *NCRTE Colloquy, 2*(2), 1–6. East Lansing: Michigan State University.

Kennedy, M. M. (1989b). Kenneth Zeichner reflecting on reflection: Mary Kennedy interviews Kenneth Zeichner. *NCRTE Colloquy, 2*(2), 15–21. East Lansing: Michigan State University.

Kennedy, M. M. (1991, Spring). An agenda for research on teacher learning. *NCRTE Special Report*, 1–27. East Lansing: Michigan State University.

Kolbert, E. (1987, Spring). Getting teachers off on the right foot. *New York Times Educational Supplement*, pp. 24–26.

Lacey, C. (1977). *The socialization of teachers*. London: Methuen.

Lampert, M. (1985). How do teachers manage to teach? *Harvard Educational Review, 55*, 178–194.

Lao-Tzu. (1963). *Tao te ching*. New York: Penguin.

Levinson, D. J. (1978). *The seasons of a man's life*. New York: Ballantine.

Lagana, J. (1970). *What happens to the attitudes of beginning teachers*. Danville, IL: Interstate Printers and Publishers.

Lightfoot, S. (1983). *The good high school*. New York: Basic Books.

Lortie, D. C. (1966). *Teacher socialization: The Robinson Crusoe model. The real world of the beginning teacher*. Washington, DC: National Commission on Teacher Education and Professional Standards.

Lortie, D. C. (1975). *Schoolteacher*. Chicago: University of Chicago Press.

McDonald, J. (1986). Raising the teacher's voice and the ironic role of theory. *Harvard Educational Review, 56*, 355–378.

Mead, G. (1938). *The philosophy of the act*. Chicago: University of Chicago Press.

Miller, P. (1964). *Errand in the wilderness*. New York: Harper & Row.

National Education Association. (1967). *The American public school teacher 1965–66*. Washington, DC: Research Division.

New York Trust Co. v. Eisner, 256 U.S. 345, 349 (1921).

Peters, R. (1960). *Authority, responsibility and education*. New York: Eriksson-Taplinger.

Pharr, H. J. (1974). A study of skills and competencies identified as problem areas for beginning and experienced teachers (Doctoral dissertation, University of Northern Colorado, 1974). *Dissertation Abstracts International, 35*, 05–A.

Powell, A., Farrar, E., & Cohen, D. K. (1985). *The shopping mall high school*. Boston: Houghton Mifflin.

Rosenholtz, S. J. (1987). Workplace conditions of teacher quality and commitment: Implications for the design of teacher induction programs. In G. A. Griffin & S. Millies (Eds.), *The first years of teaching* (pp. 15–34). Chicago: University of Illinois at Chicago.

Rousseau, J. J. (1979). *Emile* (A. Bloom, Trans.). New York: Basic Books. (Original work published 1762)

Sacks, S., & Brady, B. (1985, April). *Who teaches the city's children? A study of New York City first-year teachers*. Paper presented at the annual meeting of the American Education Research Association, Chicago.

Sarason, S. (1971). *The culture of school and the problem of change*. Boston: Allyn & Bacon.

Schön, D. (1983). *The reflective practitioner*. New York: Basic Books.

Schön, D. (1987). *Educating the reflective practitioner*. San Francisco: Jossey-Bass.

Schön, D. (1988). Coaching reflective teaching. In P. Grimmett & G. L. Erickson (Eds.), *Reflection in teacher education* (pp. 19–29). New York: Teachers College Press.

Schumacher, E. F. (1973). *Small is beautiful: Economics as if people mattered*. New York: Harper & Row.

Shulman, J. H., & Colbert, J. A. (1987). *The mentor teacher casebook*. San Francisco: Far West Laboratory for Educational Research and Development.

Shulman, J. H., & Colbert, J. A. (1988). *The intern teacher casebook*. San Francisco: Far West Laboratory for Educational Research and Development.

Sizer, T. (1984). *Horace's compromise*. New York: Houghton Mifflin.

Smith, P. (1990). *Killing the spirit: Higher education in America*. New York: Viking Press.

Stoddart, T., & Feiman-Nemser, S. (1988). Albuquerque Public Schools/University of New Mexico Graduate Intern/Teacher Induction Program Site Report. *Dialogues in teacher education* (Issue Paper 88-4), 83–90. East Lansing: Michigan State University.

Strom, S. M. (1989). The ethical dimension of teaching. In M. C. Reynolds (Ed.),

Knowledge base for the beginning teacher (pp. 267–276). New York: Pergamon Press.

Thelen, H. (1973). Profession anyone? In D. J. McCarty (Ed.), *New perspectives on teacher education* (pp. 194–213). San Francisco: Jossey-Bass.

Tobin, K. G. (1990, April). *Constructivist perspectives on teacher change.* Invited address presented at the annual meeting of the American Educational Research Association, Boston.

Travers, E. F., & Sacks, S. R. (1987). *Teacher education and the liberal arts: The position of the consortium for excellence in teacher education* (Occasional Paper). Middletown, CT: Consortium for Excellence in Teacher Education.

Vailliant, G. (1977). *Adaptation to life.* Boston: Little Brown.

Veenman, S. (1984). Perceived problems of beginning teachers. *Review of Educational Research, 5*(2), 143–178.

Wagner, L. (1985, April). *Evaluation issues in California's mentor teacher program: Where can we go from here?* Paper presented at the annual meeting of the American Education Research Association, Chicago.

Weber, M. (1958). *Essays in sociology.* New York: Oxford University Press.

Westerhoff, J. (1987). The teacher as pilgrim. In F. S. Bolin & J. M. Falk (Eds.), *Teacher renewal* (pp. 190–201). New York: Teachers College Press.

Whitehead, A. N. (1929). *The aims of education.* New York: Macmillan.

Woods, P. (1978). Relating to schoolwork: Some pupil perceptions. *Educational Review, 80,* 167–175.

Yinger, R. J. (1987). Learning the language of practice: Implications for beginning year of teaching programs. In G. A. Griffin & S. Millies (Eds.), *The first years of teaching* (pp. 65–89). Chicago: University of Illinois at Chicago.

Zeichner, K. (1983). Factors related to the socialization of teaching. In G. Griffin & H. Hukill (Eds.), *What are the pertinent issues? Proceedings of a National Working Conference* (pp. 1–59). Austin: University of Texas at Austin, Research and Development Center for Teacher Education.

Index

About the Author

Richard H. Dollase is Director of the Middlebury College Teacher Education Program, where he has taught since 1982. Dr. Dollase received his Bachelors of Arts degree from Brown University in 1962. His interest in beginning teaching dates back to 1964, his first year of teaching at Mount Greylock Regional High School in Williamstown, Massachusetts, after he completed his Masters of Arts in Teaching degree from Wesleyan University. In 1976, he received his Ed.D. from Boston University. Dr. Dollase has taught at Wheaton College in Norton, Massachusetts, where he was chair of the Education Department. He has been a visiting professor at Louisiana State University and Brown University. He is the coauthor of a four-volume African-American studies curriculum, *Black in White America*, and has published a number of articles. He has served as project director of several National Endowment for the Humanities and National Science Foundations summer institutes and conferences on teaching and the liberal arts.